ROCKIN' A HARD PLACE

John Jeter

HUB CITY PRESS

SPARTANBURG, SC

Also by John Jeter

The Plunder Room

ROCKIN' A HARD PLACE

Flats, Sharps & Other Notes from a Misfit Music Club Owner

John Jeter

First printing, November 2012

Cover Photo: Ian Curcio
Cover design: Stephen J. Long
Interior design: Corinne Manning
Editor: Betsy Teter with Chad Lawson
Proofreaders: Jill McBurney & Jan Scalisi
Printed in Saline, MI by McNaughton &
Gunn Inc.

"The Club Manager" used with permission of
Fighting Cock Press

Library of Congress Cataloging-in-
Publication Data

Jeter, John, 1960-
Rockin' a hard place : flats, sharps and
other notes from a misfit music club
owner / John Jeter.
p. cm.
 ISBN 978-1-891885-99-0 (alk. paper)
1. Jeter, John, 1960- 2. Impresarios--
South Carolina--Greenville--Biography.
3. Handlebar (Nightclub) 4. Music-
halls (Variety-theaters, cabarets, etc.)--
South Carolina--Greenville. I. Title.
ML429.J47A3 2013
792.702'3092--dc23
[B]

2012026141

ISBN 1-978-891885-99-0
E-book ISBN 1-978-891885-05-1

186 West Main Street
Spartanburg, SC 29306
864.577.9349
www.hubcity.org

To—

Kathy, who is my life,
and to Stephen, who saved it

◊
◊
◊

The Club Manager

His office is above the stage
behind a thick scarred wooden door
a desk piled high with bills, receipts
a small safe bolted to the floor
Envious friends say "Man, how sweet
to be the guy behind the Scene!"
He puts aside the payroll page —
it's time to fix the ice machine.

The overhead is suffocating;
electric, rent, insurance, beer
the mobbed-up Dumpster, glassware, liquor
mics / cables / amps / repair
advertising, ASCAP sticker
bar staff, wait staff, bouncers, sound
(the owner talks of relocating—
he might as well just burn it down)

Bands talk of blood and sweat and tears
they want more money, better dates
He knows that if they don't sell drinks
there's no point to unlock the grates
Sometimes, worn-out, alone, he thinks
'I'm through, I can't last one more week'
but reconsiders when he hears
cheers, clapping, whistles, stamping feet.

— Dave Morrison
from *Clubland*

Opening Act

The promoter knows why they're here, all those fans lining up outside the doors tonight. They file in, moving along the walls that are plastered with posters, garish bills and glossy flyers that advertise upcoming shows in black Magic Marker scrawls. He watches his customers—the ticket-buyers, the economic lifeblood of a global business whose seeds he plants right here—he watches them stop at the box-office counter and hand over their hard-earned money. They could have spent their time and treasure on a movie or a burger and beer somewhere else; he understands that. But tonight, they have come to his venue instead.

Their reasons seem to transcend the need to eat or to spend a couple of hours in a dark cinema. Almost better than anyone else in his chosen industry, the promoter knows why these people came here: to share an experience that predates films and restaurants. He convinced himself years ago that he wanted to open his own place for live music because the art form endures as a remnant of prehistoric tribal gatherings. For millennia, stories set to song have helped interpret and commemorate the human experience. That was then. Now the promoter can only hope that he will sell enough beer and booze to make music make him a living.

Inside the concert hall, big foam dice, half the size of a Smart car, dangle from the barrel roof's steel trusses. A few years ago, a friend fashioned the big ornaments as a tribute to the Rolling Stones—"Tumbling Dice." At the back end of the brick-walled room looms the large stage, with its black curtains and black sound baffles. It's dark up there, except for tiny red lights and the orange glow of decibel meters from guitar amps and from the reflective glitter of drum cymbals. The carpeted floor seems to writhe with cables and wires.

In a few moments, this space will give way to magic.

But the fans keep filling the room. Dim house lights and indeterminate music from the PA system create a familiar, even primal atmosphere. Some in the growing crowd sit, some stand, some wait to be served at the concert-hall bar. Many of them sip cold beer from a longneck bottle or a colorful cocktail from a plastic cup. Lively, anticipatory chatter gurgles through the hall.

In the booth at the far back wall, the house sound guy sits and fiddles with his Blackberry. He glances toward the stage from time to time, looking for the signal from the door off stage right. The band is still hanging out in the dressing room, tuning their instruments, talking with each other, perhaps doing something they shouldn't be doing, maybe even calming a little stage fright.

Now the house guy sees a flash, a Maglite signal from backstage. He turns around and presses a button.

The house lights fade.

The crowd erupts.

On the still-darkened stage, silhouettes begin negotiating their way through instruments and gear and take their places.

All at once, amber, crimson, blue and white lights detonate a wash of color, and the room resounds with guitars and drums and voices. Practiced and cohesive, the four people on stage, the band, sing and play song-stories to other people who are here to hear them. The melodies and rhythms hustle and flow with movement, current, even urgency.

For many of the fans, time stops, even vanishes. The promoter stops, too, but only for a moment. He feels good that more than four hundred customers fill the concert hall, the "listening room," so he allows himself a fleeting moment to savor that. Now it's up to the musicians to make the fans happy.

He returns to the office, the size of a rich man's closet. Harsh fluorescent lights shine on everything but the art that he can hear through the doors: the business of this place, the talent agencies' contracts, bills, payroll and taxes…and tomorrow night's show.

Oh, god.

He leans back in his chair and stares into the computer, where emails wait from agents who want big guarantees for their artists to play the room; from local and regional bands who just want a gig; from people "out there" who don't know much about music; he has made music his living, so he feels just a bit like the doctor who knows more than the patients do.

Thankfully, tonight's a good night. The crowd's big, the bar's making money, the bottom line will get a little boost. But tomorrow? That's a whole different ballgame. Tickets aren't just lackluster, they're almost nonexistent. He had booked tomorrow night's band months ago because he believed in the group's music and potential. But he understands now, too late, that he offered the agent too much money, a bloated guarantee for the artist to perform here. So while the staff slings drinks and fans dance and sing and the band plays on, the promoter simply stares into the void. He fears the outcome of tomorrow's show. Just about every dime he earns tonight will leave with the next tour bus twenty-four hours from now.

But, hell, at this moment? None of that matters.

He knows why they're here, the fans. They're not here because of him or the bar's cold beer and colorful cocktails, the grilled chicken sandwiches and funky artwork and show posters. They're here to share an art form that has persisted since the beginning of human history.

He won't catch any of the show tonight—he has lots of other things to do—but he's happy that the people are here. Yet, as the night slips by, he wonders, as he has so many times before, how he got himself into all of this in the first place … and why.

1

The old textile mill stood like a forgotten mausoleum. All used up after a hundred years, the abandoned factory housed only a ghost or two in its time-chipped walls. Now, though, my brother and I had other plans for this place whose red bricks had been fired from clay not far from the site of a Civil War gun factory. The first time we saw the decrepit mill, Stephen and I, a light spring breeze perfumed the air with honeysuckle and jasmine. White and pink dogwood blossoms decorated South Carolina with giddy promise. My brother and I came to look at this old factory that for decades had lured dirt-poor sharecroppers and struggling farm families to lives of urban destitution. Today, the mill was enticing us into a similar gamble with Fate. We were snooping around for a spot to start our lives in the music business.

We wound up at the old Mills Mill in Greenville because Stephen knew that I'd love the place. He knew I would agree that this would be the perfect spot for our dream, our endeavor together as brothers …our own concert hall.

The year was 1994. That year, Kurt Cobain killed himself, despite the huge success of Nirvana. O.J. Simpson was found innocent of killing other people, despite apparent evidence to the contrary. The economy was making a killing, despite "irrational exuberance" that everyone knew couldn't last. The music business was making a killing, despite the dawn of the Internet age, which would eventually convulse the music business. That summer also marked the tenth anniversary that my brother had donated his kidney and saved my life, despite the fact that doctors told my mother I wouldn't live past five.

Things seemed right with the world on that lovely spring day.

The historic mill appeared to be as full of promise as it was empty—much like our knowledge of business, *any* business, especially the music business. But as a friend told me once about learning something new: "Wanna know the best way to learn Spanish? I give you a parachute and drop you into the middle of Colombia. In a few short weeks, *su vida es fantástico!*"

A day or so before, I had driven up from Florida. At the time, I was living with my fiancée, Kathy, in St. Petersburg, where I had burned out after ten years in the newspaper game. Deliberately unemployed, I had spent the previous year "writing" and traveling—and accomplishing little more than incinerating my savings. Now, though, if my brother and I *did* find some place to open our dreamed-up music venue, I would just have to persuade Kathy to quit her newsroom job and move with me to a strange town.

What could possibly go wrong?

My brother was big, gregarious and fun-loving, with a receding hairline, a ready wit and an easygoing disposition. We had always been close, Stephen and I, born just a year and a half apart; we grew up almost as twins, Mom often dressing us the same way. Though divergent, our personalities still fit together like tongue-and-groove, not only compatible but complementary. He always operated from some elemental integrity that kept him moving, one foot in front of the other, in the "right" direction, his moral compass unshakably on target. Me, I was one of those artistic types, prone to emotional fits while flailing away at whatever distracted my footloose curiosity and uncontrollable imagination. He had always been the thoughtful, responsible, respectable type, a solid family man who was also the baby of our own family—the species that knows no natural enemies. Generous, even gullible, Stephen always put his huge heart in all the right places. In short, while I asked "why?", he asked "when?"

Stephen had moved to Greenville after graduating from nearby Wofford College, where his antics at Sigma Alpha Epsilon had become the stuff of mythos. My brother had been a model fraternity man, who, having spent three days on the frat-house sofa while he drained a keg of beer and pit-barbequed a whole pig, had ideal experience for helping run a business that essentially throws a party three or four nights a week.

For months, Stephen had cased several potential locations. He knew his way around town, having lived for the past decade in Greenville, an Upstate city of some fifty-eight thousand souls. He was married now, and he and his wife, Melanie, had a spunky six-year-old daughter, Madison. He zeroed in on Mills Mill, in part, he said, because it was so funky, in part because he liked the landlord, an affable old blueblood physician, and in part because the good doctor had told him the rent would be cheap—and he would help finance our move-in costs.

That afternoon, as my brother drove me to the mill, I was immediately wowed by the cupola that crowned the four red-brick stories. A rusting silver water tower rose near a smokestack that soared over all the rest.

Stephen pulled his gray Ford Taurus into the vast parking lot, whose cracking asphalt zigzagged with healthy weeds. Only a few cars were parked near the faded blue awning marking the entrance, which happened to be in the rear of the factory—itself hard enough to find; the mill also abutted one of the poorest, most violent neighborhoods in town. Perhaps that's when we should have given some thought to retail's First Commandment: Location. Location. Location.

After studying the ominous building for several minutes, we moved toward the darkened lobby. Feral cats skittered around piles of bricks surrounding the base of the sky-etching chimney. I noticed some activity through new windows that had been built into several of the corbelled-arch frames; the rest of the building remained bricked up, a reminder that air-conditioning had ultimately been installed—and making the mill look like one big sarcophagus.

"Does anyone actually work in here?" I asked. "I mean, are there, like, any *businesses* or anything?"

"Not really, to be honest," he said, "but this is really cool, you've gotta see this."

"Except for the obvious fact that this was once a mill, did this old place actually used to *be* anything, other than, y'know . . . abandoned?"

"They called it 'Mills Centre' for a few years, one of those flea market-type places. Now a doctor and a group of other investors own it, but they haven't done much with it."

Apparently.

The building was shaped like a backwards **E**, with the middle bar being the rear-entrance awning. Newish red bricks advertised that the mill's southern wing had been a somewhat recent addition. The space he wanted me to see was in the opposite corner, clearly the oldest, most neglected part of the structure.

"We're heading to that section over there," he said. "You'll go nuts when you see this."

The place was beginning to fire my curiosity the way the old bricks here had been fired from the red clay pulled off the banks of nearby Brushy Creek. As a history buff and recovering journalist, I grew anxious to know as much as I could about the place, my hot-wired senses lighting up.

I soaked up the story as fast as I could: In 1898, one Capt. Otis Prentiss Mills was a Confederate officer-turned-entrepreneur who knew as much about business as we did. In a cautionary prologue to our own story, Mills' eponymous company struggled for the first six years, manufacturing fine cotton sheets, twills and satins. Still, he ultimately built a mill village, comprised of four-room clapboard bungalows that now housed inner-city poverty. Within spitting distance was the sandlot field where "Shoeless" Joe Jackson once played textile-league baseball. And some time after the turn of the twentieth century, so legend has it, an eleven-year-old boy was impaled on a machine; folks insisted that "Spindle Boy" still haunted the fourth floor. The mill finally ceased operations in 1979, as the South's textile industry died. More than a dozen years later, Mills Centre failed, and our prospective landlord built a single model condominium on the topmost story. The idea was to attract buyers who would snap up dozens of these loft apartments on spec and provide the mill's ownership group with enough money to build more. We bought that optimism, too, believing that if condos really *did* open upstairs, the property's value would explode, and the mill itself might become easier to find.

"I actually used to come here when this place was Mills Centre," Stephen said, "and it used to be packed, vendors everywhere, shoppers all over the place."

"Oh? So what happened? All that just disappeared?"

"Well, see, Waccamaw Pottery opened out on the interstate a few years ago, and that's where everyone went. The mill's been pretty much closed ever since."

Anymore, he said, only a handful of businesses occupied the first two floors. The third floor remained empty. We could take the building's single elevator up there if we wanted to.

We walked into the tawdry lobby, with its faux-marble Art Deco floor and ratty acoustic-tile ceiling. Most of the fluorescent lights didn't work. The walls were painted battleship gray. I was struck by a large, black-and-white picture, framed in stained plywood. The grainy old image showed three men, one in a bowler hat, posing in front of a looming textile machine.

The buzz of history again tickled my imagination. Working in this factory, I thought, must have been hell. Before any AC was ever turned on, slatted windows were all that separated the Piedmont's viscous summer air from thousands of machines that generated even more heat. At the same time, the looms, some as big as school buses, churned at deafening decibel levels.

Stephen and I eased our way into the cool, dark hallway of the silenced mill. I was stopped by the lingering aroma of cotton lint, which still clung to the muscular heart-pine beams that lined the wood-slatted ceilings. The fragrance reminded me of a room in my grandparents' old house, where the "help" used to do the ironing.

Immediately to our left was the only place that operated on the first floor. Through windowed panels that enclosed the business from the rest of the empty hall, I saw a glistening barbershop. The mill's original flooring—pine or, I supposed, oak or maple—had been refinished with a sparkling varnish. Modern track lighting brightened the spots where the sun wasn't blasting through new windows. The handsome salon had only a couple of customers that day. All of them were African-American men.

"Black barbershop," my brother said in passing. "It hasn't been here long, but the owner, you'd like him, he's a great guy."

"Black" barbershop?

That's the moment I realized that we were planning to open a concert hall in a town whose past was riddled with racial intrigues. Greenville remained as segregated as most other Southern cities. The percentage of African-Americans hovered around the same as that of the rest of the country. Black folks simply didn't mingle much with whites here. On one side was the Reverend Jesse Jackson, a Greenville native, and on the other, Bob Jones University, which in 1975 had prohibited interracial dating and marriage. Before that, Greenville appeared in *The New Yorker* in 1947, when Dame Rebecca West covered a trial that saw thirty-one white men acquitted in the lynching of Willie Earle, a twenty-four-year-old black kid who'd supposedly robbed, then fatally stabbed, a white cab driver.

I peered past the barbershop into the long hallway that led toward the northeast corner. The only light shone from weak, intermittently operating fluorescent tubes dangling from the ceiling.

"Where's the landlord?" I asked.

"I have no idea, but he said it was fine if we made ourselves at home. He's retired, y'know, but he seems pretty busy most of the time."

Stephen went on to tell me about the genteel old physician who lived in a stately home, less than two miles away from the mill and its village. The doctor and his wife lived just on the other side of Mills Avenue in Greenville's moneyed Augusta Road neighborhood. That's where the mill owners, foremen, lawyers, doctors and other white-collar leaders spent their expanding wealth on majestic columned homes with wrought-iron fences, endless porches, perfect lawns that blinked with fireflies and clicked with mint juleps amid towering oak and magnolia trees.

The doctor, I learned, was one of several owners, a small syndicate of similarly credentialed gentlemen who had bought the mill as an investment. They were looking for tenants.

"*Actively* looking?" I asked.

Stephen shrugged, as much to me as to the abundance of empty space. At least, we had plenty of raw square footage to choose from. But before we ventured farther into the mill's shadowy first floor, we took the elevator up to the second.

We found that one of the spaces had been converted to a graphic-design studio, where we met a charming, gray-bearded artist named John Antonio. He told me with no small pride that he had created

Clemson University's iconic logo, the ubiquitous orange tiger paw. In the adjacent space was an expansive art gallery, whose owners, Patty and Richard Riley, welcomed us with no small hope that we would actually move in to the mill. It turned out that Richard's father, Dick Riley, was serving at the time as U.S. Education Secretary for President Bill Clinton.

Satisfied that we wouldn't have to worry about the neighbors, we went back downstairs. We wandered down the long main hallway, only to find a heavy metal door sealing off the eight-thousand square feet where we would build our concert hall, bar and café; the space actually happened to be *two* separate sections—ideal for the division we wanted between our revenue-generating "nightclub" and our decidedly artistic "Listening Room." We slid open the door on its rails, and a rope-and-weight pulley system kept it open behind us.

We found ourselves in a room filled with dusty light. Here, too, the bricks had been blown from the molds and were replaced with windows whose flimsy mullions barely held panes that were cracked or shattered. The windows looked out on the mill's creepy, narrow back alley.

A couple of rows of columns, which looked like ancient telephone poles, bolstered the ten- to twelve-foot-high ceilings. The ceilings, in turn, supported floors that could withstand looms that shook with the power of locomotives. (Little did we know, until much later, that these same floors could easily bear the weight of several hundred young rock 'n' roll fans, all jumping up and down in unison to their favorite songs.) Here, the ruddy brick-and-wood ambiance felt ideal for a tucked-away bistro.

"In fact," Stephen said, "this area used to be the snack bar for Mills Centre."

It would be easy enough, then, to build a small kitchen against the far wall over there, and serve some light food over here before the shows. The open space could likely seat forty or fifty people.

We walked around "our café" for a few minutes, until I followed my brother into a windowless hall that ramped down into . . .

"...oh... my...god," I said, gazing up and around the sun-lighted dilapidation.

Goosebumps.

The ceiling vaulted at least twenty feet. The room felt like a cathedral. Broad squares of light fell through windows that were also in various states of disrepair.

"Is this cool or what, huh?"

The big square box opened on two sides—perfect exits for an assembly hall and for bands to load in their gear; the door to the left opened up next to the old smokestack. Arched windows towered over the two doors, adding even more light to the room.

The walls, which also were two-feet thick here, making the concert hall virtually soundproof, had been covered with some sort of plaster or mortar, chunks of which had fallen off over time. (One evening a few months later, a blue-haired maven constructively commented, "My, these walls...look ...so...un-*finish*'d.") We thought the mottled walls looked pretty sweet, so we left them that way.

Shattered glass and spilled paint, industrial gunk and petrified bird shit carpeted the floor. I tapped my foot and asked, "What's under here?"

"Oh, down there, that used to be the boiler room for the whole mill." We glanced toward the chimney. "You saw the creek that runs along the parking lot."

I did. That must have been where the mill sucked up the water to feed its steam-powered electrical generators.

In silent awe, we traded smiles.

Yes!

He had found the ideal space. These rooms exuded the kind of cutting-edge and hyper-funky ambience that would make this town sit up and take notice—assuming, of course, that anyone could *find* the place.

Unfazed and enchanted, I said, "Dude, this reminds me of SoHo, total New York chic. And the intimacy in here"—I clapped my hands, as if I knew the first thing about acoustics—"the *sound* is going to be awesome."

He beamed with pride at his off-the-beaten-path discovery. "Oh, yeah, bro, this whole thing is going to be awesome."

From the top corner nearest the smokestack, a sudden fluttering startled the hell out of us.

"What the—?" I ducked from the commotion.

"Whoa!" My brother pointed to gaping holes in the walls and ceiling and at the busted windows where pigeons had made themselves at home.

"Well, okay," I said. "I guess it's going to take a little fixing up."

He crossed his arms and nodded. We'd worry about that later, along with the money neither of us had to undertake such an operation.

Even Ecclesiastes would tell you that your every idea is nothing but vanity, that someone out there has already thought of it and done it—except perhaps for the first moonwalk, building the Titanic or being the first person to gulp an oyster. So, yes, vanity of vanities, my brother and I believed that his hometown and, soon, mine, could use our special touch in a concert hall. But, *Ecclesiastically* speaking, our idea—half-baked as it was because nobody actually *thinks* an idea All The Way Through—came from *somewhere*. Ours came from McDibb's, a magical listening room in the heart of Black Mountain, a two-hour drive away, in western North Carolina.

Black Mountain is one of those towns that make you think that you've accidentally returned to the '60s. Or perhaps you were aiming for Sedona, Arizona, but wound up in the Blue Ridge Mountain foothills instead. Black Mountain and environs are said to be dotted with "vortices"—spiritualists' bioelectric healing power points—and more of them than anywhere else on Earth. No wonder, then, that McDibb's had found a harmonious conjunction with the community.

Most folks know Black Mountain as the home of Roberta Flack, the Rev. Billy Graham (actually from the adjacent suburb of Montreat) and the Light Center, a geodesic dome where you can reset your mind, body and spirit under an array of colored lighting. Black Mountain College, before it closed in 1957, was a renowned arts school whose faculty included the likes of Willem and Elaine de Kooning and whose guest lecturers numbered Albert Einstein and William Carlos Williams.

McDibb's was founded in 1978, and even while it remained in operation, the little room had created its own magnetic mystique. The owners ran an intimate, bohemian salon for performers, poets and patrons.

The space was a simple brick box. The stage was small; you could put your feet up on it if you happened to nab one of the folding chairs in the front row. The mascot was a rat. The atmosphere felt warm and cozy and included local *objets d'art*; bits of nostalgia, including the cookstove from the landmark café that McDibb's had replaced; hippie chicks nursing their newborns; and, of course, dogs, the *de rigueur* companions of the McDibb's' batik-wrapped fans.

David Peele, one of the owners, helped power all that. He had dubbed McDibb's a "listening room," pretty much before anyone in the Deep South knew what one was. He also kept his bar and performance area smoke-free—unheard of in tobacco country. He booked top-flight talent, too, including, to name but a few: bluesman Taj Mahal; Townes Van Zandt; Doc Watson; John Hartford, the banjo player most famous for "Gentle On My Mind"; and a young fiddler named Alison Krauss.

Stephen took me to McDibb's several times. We had always loved music, especially the *live* kind. My parents had taken us to our first Broadway show when I was eight years old; we saw Danny Kaye in *Two By Two*. They took us to see Johnny Cash and Up With People! (remember them?). Stephen and I had seen Pete Seeger and Arlo Guthrie at the famed Wolf Trap Farm Park near Washington, D.C. We were Jimmy Buffett fans. I attended my first rock concert at a velodrome in then-West Germany, where Alice Cooper staged his *Welcome To My Nightmare*. I was fourteen at the time, and a year later, I sat in the second row at a sold-out Cat Stevens concert in a German arena. In my adulthood, I saw Bruce Springsteen more times than I could count; Georg Solti conducting Mahler's Symphony No. 2 (Resurrection) in an intense Chicago performance; Lena Horne, Andrés Segovia, the Vienna Boys Choir and even Aretha Franklin at an Easter service in Harlem.

As for our own musical talent, only Stephen had any, a great singing voice, which he rarely used. Me, I couldn't play a contact sport. Still, my life has always been and will always be about Art, with a capital A. In my earliest memory, I wanted to write. I started with crayons, even before I learned the alphabet. And I always loved books. I didn't know much about records, per se, didn't own anything resembling a collection of vinyl, but musicals, theater, opera, rock concerts all appealed to me. For me, humanity's Art has always trumped its financial intercourse. After all, cave paintings have endured longer than any society's currency. I suppose that's why I have always felt that Art is the nobler of the two, and noble intention, however naïve, always triumphs—at least, to me it does.

Anyway, Stephen had counted on McDibb's to slake his thirst for the laid-back folk-pop that he liked best. While Greenville did have a couple of venues at the time, none particularly catered to his tastes or offered the safe, intimate, clean and grown-up atmosphere that he preferred and wanted to share with his family. Thus he believed, as so many people in so many places do, that "this town really needs a place like this!"—the same way any community that's worth its weight needs a museum.

And so he found his template and our inspiration on Cherry Street in Black Mountain.

During one of our several visits there to see Mike Cross, David Wilcox, Livingston Taylor and a few others, Stephen and I decided that, one day, we wanted to *be* McDibb's. After all, the venue's owners had built a community around his business, and we wanted that, too. We admired the McDibb's' family feel and the fact that it didn't have a backstage dressing room. The proprietors encouraged their performers, often some of the biggest names in the business, to mingle with customers, their fans.

It was during one visit to McDibb's that we decided on the name for our would-be establishment.

We would call our own listening room The Handlebar.

"Kidney" is one of those mashed-up words that stumble off the tongue like some unwanted noun in search of a bad joke—an organ that plays off-key, a human bean. The term's gauzy origin is said to be the corruption of some Middle or Old English word for "womb" or "egg," which seems particularly poignant here.

In 1984, a long time ago, my brother gave me his kidney. My own medical history's long and too weird to get into, but suffice to say that shortly after I graduated from college, my sole surviving kidney failed. At the time, I was a young newspaperman in San Antonio, Texas. My family rallied round. Tests were taken. Medical histories were examined. Determinations were made. My brother turned out to be a perfect match—an almost foregone conclusion considering that we'd grown up as close to twins as brothers can be without having been born a few minutes' apart.

I didn't formally ask him for his kidney. He didn't actually say, in so many words, that he would be the one to donate it, either. The whole thing just sort of...happened. It was as if the transplant that everyone in our family—my sister, my brother, my parents and me—all knew was coming finally came, and the solution to the problem was already there: Stephen. It's not that anybody took anyone else's decisions lightly or for granted, or that everyone just assumed that my brother would be delighted to sacrifice one of his body parts, nothing like that. No, the process just seemed as natural as getting married or having children or dying, and since nobody wanted the latter to happen to me, well, Stephen just went ahead and gave me the rest of my life. No questions or drama, just unspoken, unwavering, unconditional love.

On a broiling-hot summer afternoon, we entered the hospital together.

Early on July 24, 1984, orderlies wheeled him into one operating room and me into another. Before the anesthesiologist knocked me out, I looked into the eyes of the surgeon and said, dazed and doped, "Goodnight, sweet prince."

When they opened up my brother's right flank, doctors found a kidney the size of a basketball. They had to remove one of his ribs to get it out. And they had to stuff it hard into my abdomen, just to the north of my bladder.

Long, agonizing hours later—for my family, not for me; I was in Narcotic Wonderland—my brother was back in his room, and I was in the ICU with maddening and irritating cannulae snaking from various parts of my body.

Well into that first evening, the oddly placed kidney still wouldn't function. Nothing was happening. The surgeon counseled patience and hope to my parents' frustration and fear, while I, in drugged-out discomfort, simply slurred: "Take this fucking tube out of my nose and give me a cold beer, and I'll pee like crazy."

Finally, of course, relief and so forth began to flow; Stephen's kidney became mine. During the next two-and-a-half days that he remained with me in the hospital, we flirted with the nurses, and he incited surgical-glove water-balloon fights and wheelchair races. Always on the lookout for fun and always wanting to lighten up any heavy situation, my brother also suggested that, during our recuperation, we start a mustache-growing contest.

Soon enough, my upper lip sprouted a handlebar.

Exactly ten years later, as naturally as the moment it was decided that my brother would save my life, so it seemed just as appropriate to honor our dream with his gift.

⋮

While we stood inside the old mill's hindmost shell, where we envisioned our concert hall, we became even more determined to open an intimate and unique concert hall. In fact, we already were, in our minds anyway, booking bands and whipping ourselves into a music-fan frenzy.

"Dude," he said, whapping my arm, "The Mavericks!"

I offered him a puzzled look, if only because I just couldn't picture a band the size and stature of The Mavericks squeezed into what would have to be a very small stage in that space available here. "Sure, okay, if we can get them."

"Flaco Jimenez! We gotta get Flaco Jimenez!"

Okay, he lost me there. Flaco Jimenez?

"I love to say that name!"

Flaco Jimenez was a Tejano accordionist and one of Texas's most treasured pioneers, and he later joined The Mavericks on the band's most successful single, "All You Ever Do Is Bring Me Down." But did anybody in the Upstate even know who Flaco Jimenez *was*? So, all of a sudden, right then and there, I started to think like a promoter; unknowingly, I had made my first step toward the slippery slope where the purity of art plunges into the valley of debt.

"Arlo Guthrie!" I said.

Of course! Arlo! The idea was a no-brainer; we would *definitely* get him.

"Hootie and the Blowfish!" he said. Hootie, hailing from nearby Columbia, was on the verge of releasing *Cracked Rear View*, which went on to sell sixteen million copies and become the fifteenth best-selling American album of all time.

"Greg Brown!" I said. "John Gorka! Patty Larkin!" I had learned about them in Tampa, where I was addicted to WMNF, the public-radio station that played a long block of folk music every morning. From Tampa's powerful NPR station, I soaked up John Gorka, Rod MacDonald, Dar Williams, Cheryl Wheeler, Christine Lavin and her Four Bitchin' Babes—all part of the New Folk revival. Those artists and that genre would be my wheelhouse, I knew even then, with maybe some blues thrown in, if only because I was familiar with Robert Johnson.

Stephen and I looked at each other and simultaneously said, "Roy Book Binder!"

Now we were cooking. The acoustic-blues guitarist and story-teller with the bushy mustache knew everything anyone could want to know about South Carolina legends Rev. Gary Davis and Pink Anderson, from whom Pink Floyd drew half their name. Roy would be a great catch, not just for his talent but for his connections, such as they were, to the region.

Of course, our visions and fantasies were limited by the fact that we had no clue how to go about getting any of them to play our dream venue. How did you actually *book* someone like Arlo Guthrie or The Mavericks for your room? How much would artists like those two cost? Who would you call? Agents? And how would you go about finding *them*? How did all this work, the entire machinery of the music business?

That pretty spring day, my brother and I didn't stop to concern ourselves with any of that stuff. We were too busy congratulating ourselves on his blockbuster real-estate discovery and on our brilliant booking ideas. And when we finally returned to his car, we further envisioned the old mill bustling with ticket-buyers and *our* space filled with unforgettable shows.

2

What a way to start a lifelong partnership: Quit your job; persuade your betrothed to abandon her career; get married; take a six-week honeymoon drive in a crammed Honda; return home; move your entire household to an unfamiliar town; and open your own small business—all in about three months. Oh, and we're not talking about just any small business, but a live-music venue, a risky venture, at best, in an industry that the three of us knew absolutely nothing about.

That didn't stop my brother and me from working up a business plan whose wild-eyed enthusiasm was matched only by its unfounded optimism and astonishing ignorance. In our formal blueprint, we dubbed our new company Handlebar Enterprises Inc., which, as they say in business jargon, was d/b/a—or "doing business as"—THE HANDLEBAR: A LISTENING ROOM. We rocked our presentation with fancy (and costly) spreadsheets, a Profit & Loss Statement and Projections and a zippy narrative; I was a writer, after all. With our inch-thick plan in hand and our decision—without Kathy—to pursue a lease at the old mill, he and I decided that we would open for business on September 30, 1994.

Until Kathy and I married on July 18, we were still living in Florida. She was busy working and planning our small and, yes, tasteful wedding, while I mapped out our epic cross-country honeymoon. Sometime in there, we made a quick trip to Greenville to join Stephen in signing our lives away on a five-year lease for our space in the mill, which amounted to about four percent of the massive building.

As the days rolled toward our marriage, and the reality of our new business commitment sank in, Kathy and I found an entirely new avenue of tension ramping up between us. Never mind that matrimony just by itself can cause a little stress, we were now involved in serious conversations about a future as uncertain as any faced by unprepared parents.

The day after Kathy and I exchanged vows, we left on our trip.

Our itinerary would take us from St. Petersburg, along the Gulf Coast and into Texas, all the way to San Diego. From there, we would dip down to Baja, California, for a few days, then head up California's Highway 1 and into the Great Northwest. After turning right into British Columbia, we would ultimately meander back to Florida.

Along the way we stopped in Santa Fe, New Mexico. We instantly became enchanted with the brown-stucco homes festooned with pastel-blue shutters and strands of red chili peppers; all those *luminaria* and twinkling lights; the food and festive, artsy ambience.

The afternoon that we arrived, we picked up the local entertainment paper and read that Tish Hinojosa was going to play at a club later that night, a place called Luna.

I had never seen Tish before, but I owned a couple of her records. I loved her music and had something of a crush on the pretty, silver-throated songwriter. In those days, Tish was riding high—for a Mexican-American folk singer, anyway—with a new album and rave reviews that compared her with Emmylou Harris.

We arrived at Luna while the hot summer sun was still shining.

The club was big and airy, with a capacity that had to exceed two-thousand, or so we guessed. The large stage sat against the rear wall, a huge bar ran along a side wall, and a mezzanine offered several pool tables. Televisions blinked over high-topped tables that skirted the wide, concrete floor. The high-ceilinged room looked like a cross between a honky-tonk, sports bar and airplane hangar.

In the big awkward emptiness, Kathy and I kept moving around, trying to find a place where we could hear Tish over the *click-clack* of billiard balls and the silent distraction of all those TVs.

While Tish and her band played to the scattered handful of people, Kathy and I watched a young man pace all over the club, as conspicuous as a debutante at a truck stop. He was short, square-ly built, dark-haired and scruffy, and he wore khaki cargo shorts, a loose-fitting T-shirt, hiking boots with thick beige socks. A fanny pack drooped from his belly.

During the band's set break, when most everyone else had taken the opportunity to flee, I tracked him down to extract some valuable intel, grab a few insider tips on what running a business like this was really like.

He introduced himself as the promoter.

Even then, the term left an unsavory taste on my tongue. The word smacked of big hair and big schemes. I could picture only a shady con artist whose singular goal was to separate fun-seeking innocents from their disposable income. A "promoter" was a P.T. Barnum or a Don King, a savvy and smarmy expert at exploiting entertainers for extravagant sums. The job title alone sounded shady, somehow even criminal. Yet it never occurred to me, even while we were planning our concert venture, that I would actually *become* one, too. But if I were to be a promoter, I told myself even then, I would be different. Oh, no, I wouldn't be some drunken, strung-out, money-driven scumbag. My job would be to present great artists in a room that wanted great art as much as I did.

"Not much of a crowd tonight," I said, stating the painfully obvi-ous.

"Yeah." He grimaced. "But the Smashing Pumpkins are playing here next week."

He had every right to sound boastful. The year before, Billy Corgan and his punk/new wave band had released their breakthrough album, *Siamese Dream*. Now their cachet was huge. Tonight, Luna may have been getting its ass kicked, but next week might make up for all the money that would soon walk out the door with Tish's road manager. Even I could see the math in all that. Still, it was fun to envision a couple thousand people packing out this joint, drinking the bar dry, running the staff into the ground and infusing the club with cash.

"Smashing Pumpkins. Nice," I said. "That should do well."

"Tickets are selling pretty good."

Scary thoughts should have been fluttering through my brain like so many rabid bats. This guy's getting slaughtered here! He's got thousands of square feet worth of mortgage, a bunch of idle employees and a sound guy and, oh, yeah, a pretty damned expensive artist. He's not about to pull a bunch of cash right out of his ass, now is he? Don't you see? Yes, how would I feel if I were in his steel-toed shoes? How would I handle a financial beating? What kind of emotional or even spiritual toll would that sort of thing take on me, if any? And how would our business fare if we ever took a hit like the one his club was taking that night? And yet, I just envied this guy's on-the-job wardrobe and how cool it must to hang out with the likes of Tish Hinojosa—enraptured with the idea that the lovely singer/songwriter would soon be standing on a stage…in a concert hall…of my very own!

I asked the promoter how to get in touch with Ms. Hinojosa, and he directed me to her road manager, who was closeted near the club's front door. He was manning a boutique's worth of merchandise—CDs, concert T-shirts and other swag—and selling all of it to precisely no one.

He and I chatted briefly and amiably, until he proffered a business card with her contact information: the William Morris Agency. Now that sounded like a big deal!

With all the confidence of a Girl Scout selling cookies at a Hell's

Angels rally, I waved my hand toward the band. "Say, uh, how much would Tish charge for a show like this?"

"Oh, you'd have to ask her agent."

I couldn't wait. I was all kinds of excited to try negotiating with some influential enchilada at some powerful and byzantine empire the likes of the vaunted, century-old William Morris Agency.

In fact, I had already flirted with one agent, even though he just worked for a much smaller and, therefore, more accessible agency. Before Kathy and I left for our honeymoon, I had sent off a breathless letter of breathtaking guilelessness to the agency that represented the dream act we hoped to get for our Grand Opening:

> We're really excited about The Handlebar, and, as I mentioned to you, we're looking forward to making our venue one of the finest entertainment experiences in the Upstate of South Carolina . . . and beyond. So we're pretty anxious to start filling our calendar—with practically everyone on your list: Ani DiFranco to The Flirtations *[who?]* to Tom Paxton. Just say the word.
>
> To recap what I told you about us, THE HANDLEBAR: A LISTENING ROOM will have a top-of-the-line sound system *[we would?]*, with wash lighting *[wash lighting?]*. Our bar area is separate from the music hall, which will have a capacity of about 300 seats *[really?]*; that separation means absolutely no distraction for the artists: Our intent is to serve music, not a full menu. *[!]*

Yes, I was admitting right out of the box that I was no "real" promoter, with the instincts and skills to survive in the industry, and that it still hadn't occurred to me that the business of music turned almost exclusively on money.

While Kathy and I continued driving through some of North America's most awe-inspiring scenery, we spent hours discussing our developing enterprise.

Mostly, we argued.

Our bickering generally stemmed from the constant phone calls that we received from my brother just about everywhere we went. Remember, these were the days before cell phones, smart phones, text messages and Wi-Fi, so we stopped whenever and wherever we could, in the desert, at diners and in truck-stop payphones and interstate rest areas. Kathy and I had been gone barely two weeks before Stephen began begging us to cut our trip short, pleading for us to return as fast as we could, to return home—never mind that we still hadn't moved our belongings to South Carolina; Greenville wasn't even "home" yet for us. He often called several times a day, leaving messages at campgrounds and motels along our route, to tell us about the latest crisis.

He had every right to be panicked. He had spent the last several weeks distributing our nifty business plan and arranging for massive and multiple loans. Now some financing began coming in, along with plans and promissory notes. All three of us, then, would have to be together to sign reams of paperwork, most of which included the word "lien."

But my new bride and I were busy trying to have fun. Whenever we could avoid Stephen and his frantic calls, we tried to enjoy our honeymoon: a romantic meal aboard a boat, just the two of us, on the San Antonio River; a lobster dinner overlooking the Pacific Ocean in Mexico; California's majestic redwoods; fresh raspberries as big as plums in British Columbia. We even ran into one of my journalism-school classmates, Glen, who appeared out of nowhere at a *pueblo* near Taos.

All this time, Stephen somehow squeezed meetings and hearings with bankers and bureaucrats into his day job with a global snack-food conglomerate. For him, the pressure was building. So he called. A lot.

Whenever Kathy and I stopped at some payphone somewhere, my conversations with Stephen naturally involved only the two of us; Kathy was left out. The moment I hung up, though, she demanded, rightfully, to hear every word, every detail, every scrap of news, good, bad or otherwise. Being a man, I wasn't good—in fact, I was terrible—at translating for her what he had just told me about the goings-on a couple thousand miles away. All that I could ever repeat back to my wife was that we needed to abbreviate our itinerary and high-tail it back to St. Petersburg, where we could quickly pack and move to Greenville.

"Honey! Our business is going to open in less than three months! What're we supposed to do? Stephen can't handle all this stuff by himself and he shouldn't have to!"

What, she wanted to know, *was* "all this stuff," exactly?

"Sweetie, listen," I said, "Stephen says again that we really need to get back, so that we can help him with the zillions of problems involved with opening our business."

"Like *what*? I mean, like, what problems specifically. Tell me what's going on there? Everything."

Geez! Her needling questions, fueled by her insistence on knowing every single little detail, only added to our shared and mounting anxiety.

"Oh, honey, for god's sake, I don't *know*!" That was the best I could offer, especially since I'd forgotten most of what Stephen had just told me, from the cost of blueprints to whether the City's design-and-preservation board had signed off on the changes we planned make to this place that was on the National Register of Historic Places. "All's I can tell you is that he says he's dealing with zillions of problems."

The tension finally boiled over in western Canada.

On a beautiful, strangely warm twilight, we settled onto the empty deck of a restaurant overlooking the remote town of Kamloops. I don't recall the specifics of our argument, mostly because we likely fought over something petty or pointless, but it was a bad fight. In other words, I was a total asshole, passive-aggressive, dismissive and distracted.

In my defense, frankly, the only thing that I really cared about at the time, other than having fun on our honeymoon, was how we would get artists to perform at our new venue. Forget blueprints and bar glasses, what about bands? Now we had precious little time to complete the renovations and open for business. We had already signed ourselves into a quarter-million-dollar debt, so now we had to figure out how to start paying all that money back. The only way to do that was to book the artists who would pull in paying customers.

Stephen and I had long since decided on the one performer who would be perfect for our Grand Opening. Even before we gave much thought to a concert calendar that would extend much beyond the end of September, we booked Livingston Taylor. The North Carolina native and James's brother—one of our favorites from McDibb's— would play a show at eight p.m. sharp on the last Friday in September.

As far as I was concerned, then, my brother and my wife could fret to their hearts' content over furniture and fixtures, but wasn't it even *more* important to schedule *artists* for our new music room?

Panic and pressure prevailed, so we lopped off a quarter of our original route and raced back to Florida. As soon as we arrived there, a moving van hauled our belongings to Greenville, where we threw ourselves into a circus of builders, electricians, plumbers, endless trips to the hardware store and mounting legal and financial obligations.

Immediately, we started collecting kitchen and bar equipment, sound and PA gear, credit-card machines, computers...We worked nearly around the clock. We hammered and painted and purchased and planned and scurried and worried. We worked to understand the arcane mechanics of concert touring, promotion and presentation. Stephen and I combed through the industry magazine, *Pollstar*, which listed thousands of artists who were still on the road, along with the contact information for their agents and agencies. We had plenty to do before five p.m. on September 30, when everything had to be ready for the City of Greenville to issue our official Certificate of Occupancy. Without a permit, we weren't legally allowed to admit anyone into our place. No admittance meant no show. No show meant one hell of a problem.

The days raced by in a grueling blur.

When our big Grand Opening finally arrived, the dream left us drained. We were overwhelmed and terrified.

By then, Stephen and Kathy had amassed an army of friends and well-wishers to put the finishing touches on our new Handlebar.

We had a party to put on. Our show that night was sold out, or close to it.

By three-thirty that afternoon, though, I hit a wall. Wobbling in exhaustion, I begged to leave for a few minutes, so that I could go to our condo and steal a quick nap.

An hour later, I returned to amped-up chaos.

Throughout the mill's first floor, a flurry of contractors and construction workers splashed through puddles from busted sprinkler lines that wouldn't quit spraying. In the long, dark hallway between the mill's entrance and the sliding metal door to our space, plumbers and electricians worked on pipes and conduit. All the while, City inspectors and the Fire Marshal consulted their clipboards and pointed out faulty wiring and obvious leaks.

The clock ticked toward four-thirty.

Five p.m. opening—no way. No… freakin'…way.

Only the City's Fire and Building officials could sign off on our precious Certificate of Occupancy. Until every last coding issue was addressed, the iron gates of our bar area and the steel doors to our "auditorium" would remained locked, closed to the public.

I picked my way through the flood of pandemonium in the hall and walked straight into a warm, strange, glittering world. New pendant lights glowed over shiny tables. Crystal-clear Pilsner and wine glasses glistened in the rack above the bar, reflecting strings of tiny white lights that sparkled everywhere.

It was quarter to five.

The flooding pipes were finally stanched, the electrical- and plumbing-code issues apparently had been repaired to the building officials' satisfaction, and now everything depended on one man: Bob Cook.

Mr. Cook, as he preferred to be addressed, was one of the City's assistant fire chiefs. He went about his business with near-Calvinist severity. His hawk-like features, hawk-like eyes and hawk-like demeanor hovered over everything. You either burrowed into his mountains of fire-and-safety codes or you faced the consequences; his regulatory talons would shred you into oblivion.

Minutes before five, we still had no Occupancy Permit.

People skittered everywhere. My parents were about to arrive in the bus they had chartered and filled with some sixty ticket-holding friends.

Chairs packed our small theater beyond its capacity, though nobody had told us yet, formally, anyway, what our official capacity would be.

A few minutes before the appointed hour, Mr. Cook looked at me with his piercing eyes and said, "You're a lucky man, Mr. Jeter." He handed over the signed certificate.

We opened the gates.

The relief blew my last emotional gasket. I lost myself in tears, choked with pride, exhaustion, admiration, fear, excitement and…

I had to pull myself together, show some pluck and get to work.

I looked around at all the glitter, at my brother and my wife and our new staff, which included our big, gregarious bartender, Roger, and a small crew of earnest, attractive, cheerful coeds from nearby Furman University. Everybody was going about the business of doing our business.

Here they come! People are beginning to arrive! The show's sold out!
Welcome to THE HANDLEBAR: A LISTENING ROOM.

All this time, in all that bustling panic, we three had pretty much for-gotten about the one person who figured as our primary reason for opening this particular business in the first place: the artist.

Livingston Taylor had arrived earlier in the afternoon, just him and his guitar. He settled into our tiny dressing room, which sat just off stage left and included its very own bathroom; the similarly sized closet across the stage held all the amps and monitors, cables and microphones—the esoteric hardware that powered our PA.

The cornerstone of any concert hall, needless to say, is its sound. While our new system and its installation had contributed to the decimation of our construction and furniture-and-fixtures budgets, the brainiac techs who had helped us buy all that gear kept harping on us that the forty-thousand dollars we had spent was sufficient for little more than a solo folk artist. Just right for our first performer, anyway.

While everyone else hurried and scurried, I stood just inside the door that conveniently separated the kitchen from the concert hall and watched the proceedings onstage and in the sound booth. I chewed my fingernails in anxious ignorance, while our sound guy and his assistants wrestled with all that technology to make it work. They had already tweaked the system to ensure that the sound of music would actually play through it, but here, now, was the first real live test.

I watched Livingston's sound check. Goose bumps told me every-thing I needed to know about the physics of music, the dynamics of voice and instrument, the dimensions and composition of the room and all the other whiz-bang science that would forever be over my head. While our sound guy twisted knobs and pushed faders, Liv-ingston played his guitar and sang a song or two until he said he was satisfied. Then he moved to the piano.

Yes, a piano. And not just any piano. In the first artist contract that we ever signed, we had agreed to rent an acoustic piano, a baby grand, at our expense. The cost was one thing. Moving, setting and tuning the damn thing, which filled nearly half of our minuscule stage, just piled on stress where no more could fit now.

Livingston's contract also stipulated a fifty-percent payment a month in advance, the industry-standard deposit on his performance fee. We had obediently mailed a cashier's check to his agency. And on top of all that, his contract further stated that he would be paid the balance of his guarantee whether we were legally permitted to open or not, whether he played the first note or all of them.

Satisfied with the sound check and apparently happy with the sweet acoustics of this virgin venue, Livingston excused himself to the dressing room. There, he sat alone until his eight p.m. show. (We had decided against having an opening act, believing, as the music-loving purists we were, that fans came to see the marquee headliner, not some "rising" songwriter whose songs they'd never heard.)

I stood in the room now filled with total silence and too many chairs. We'd had to jam as many of them as we could into too-tight rows, despite our freshly approved capacity: two hundred-and-forty seated and three hundred-and-fifty standing. We believed that the space would and, in fact, should hold three-hundred seats, except for the inconvenient problem that so many chairs simply wouldn't fit. Regardless, we had to sell all three hundred tickets if we had any hope of breaking even on all of our show expenses: Livingston's guarantee; the piano rental; the sound guy's fee; feeding and watering the artist; ticket-printing costs; advertising and marketing; taxes ... Why, I was already beginning to think like a *real* promoter!

Contented, so far as I knew how to be, that all was right on the production side, I watched our first-ever crowd pour in. With an adrenaline-fired rush, I sat just up the ramp from the concert hall, at a beat-up old office desk, where I had appointed myself as the box-office manager. I had already muscled my way into being the "talent buyer," edging my brother away from what had to be the sexiest job in the company, if not in town. Stephen, meanwhile, found himself in the kitchen, where with few tools and only some summer-job experience he began slinging plate after plate. Kathy helped him whenever she could get away from doing everything else: managing the bar, the floor and staff, the customers and, ultimately, me.

As I sat with my cash draw and stack of tickets, my parents and their friends soon arrived. Before losing themselves in our packed house, they hugged us all, took pictures and generally beamed with pride. While they shared generously and genuinely in our achievement, I was sure that they were working hard to conceal their shattered nerves about our preposterous enterprise, never mind their investment(s) in it.

The dinner rush continued to swell. Our limited kitchen offered an equally limited menu that included our only specialty, vegetarian chili, along with black-bean nachos and sandwiches; we knew as much about opening and operating a restaurant as we did about running a music venue. We also had installed one of those old-timey dishwashers, the kind with the hand-cranked wringers, painted it white and filled the tub with salted peanuts, free bowls for everyone, so the floor was soon blanketed with shells.

As soon as Livingston gave us the go-ahead from his private perch backstage, I opened the heavy metal doors to our concert hall.

The show would start in about a half hour.

I sold tickets and tore stubs that I knew we were required to keep for our all-important records, and I watched the lifeblood of our music business begin to flow.

Soon, the house lights dimmed. The overcrowded room took on an extraordinary air of darkened, even romantic, intimacy and burbling anticipation.

I worked my way through the crammed-in seats, where I darted into the dressing room to see if Livingston was ready. He smiled and nodded and strapped on his guitar.

"I'll introduce you, if that's okay, if you want me to say anything in particular. Oh, and as soon as I say your name, if you could close the dressing-room door or turn off the light here"—I flipped the switch—"so that it doesn't spill out onto the stage."

Stepping out under the bright, multicolored lights, I was greeted with warm applause. And then I did the best I could to hold myself together while I introduced…

Tonight, live from The Handlebar, ladies and gentlemen, please welcome Livingston Taylor!

His polished charm and sweet playfulness washed over the audience. His songs seemed to move everyone the same way they had moved my brother and me at McDibb's, the way I hoped to move people with art that I couldn't make myself.

During his set, he sang an amusing ditty about a dollar bill that makes a roundabout and, of course, implausible, journey from an unnamed woman to her lover. In the cleverly titled "Dollar Bill Song," the woman scrawls "I love you" next to George Washington's picture, then spends the buck at a grocery store. The bill gets passed from a Laundromat to a poker game to a rabbi to a junkie and a liquor-store holdup, until finally making its way to the woman's sweetheart, who races to a phone to tell her that he had gotten her message.

Watching Livingston Taylor perform on our very own stage that night, I felt that this new Handlebar was sending a message, too—that our hard-earned hopes and lofty business-plan dreams would come true.

As soon as the show ended and the house lights went up, a few folks lingered in the bar. Most of them, we hoped, went home happy, delighted in their discovery of this new place that had showed them a good time. For me, the adrenaline began to drain away, while fatigue-tempered exhilaration dissolved the anxiety of all those frenzied hours before. We had seen the dollar bill come back to us.

At around eleven, we asked Livingston to sit down with us and share a cup of coffee or a drink and tell us what he thought about his experience, our room, our future, what we did right, what we'd done wrong.

With his quirky smile and the patrician wisdom of a veteran performer, he offered fairly good reviews, sounding relaxed, yet earnest and sincere. Things apparently had gone well.

"You *do* know," he told us, "that you all are at the bottom of the food chain, right? That is, the, uh, pecking order in the music industry."

"How's that?" I asked.

"Well, in the music business, you have the agent, who basically works Monday through Friday, takes no risks, goes home every night, and makes his living off the artist. The agent sits at the top of the heap." Livingston leaned against his chair and draped one leg over the other, lacing his hands together and resting them on his knee. "Next, you have the artist's manager or management team, but you won't ever get to talk with them. They handle the artist and work almost exclusively behind the scenes. Then you have the artist, who is on the road all the time and takes plenty of risk because he never knows if he's going to arrive at a venue that's padlocked. He also sings his heart out, and at the end of the night, he may—or may not—get paid, and usually not very well… "

I silently chafed at that. It seemed to me that anyone who earned in one day what I used to make in one month at my last newspaper job was pulling down some stout cheddar—a day's work that included some travel, a half-hour sound check and two hours of playing.

"… and then the artist stays by himself in hotel a room night after night." He paused and looked around at our ever-slackening faces. "And, finally, you have the promoter, who takes all the risk and works all the time. Forget about the whole music-business part, everyone knows that just running a *restaurant* requires a twenty-four/seven commitment."

You could almost see and hear our collective gulp.

"Okay," I said, "but what about booking artists, bands? I mean, you mention the agents . . . " With the help of *Pollstar* and the telephone, in those clunky days before email and the Internet, I had already begun reaching out to agents and agencies, feeling my way through the labyrinth, trying to make contacts, build relationships, I supposed, and learn how all this stuff worked. Sure, we had already booked a number of artists—some of my favorites, too!

"Keep in mind that agents are out there to get the best gigs possible for their clients, the artists on their roster, at the biggest possible commission they can get, which all simply means that you have to be really careful."

Too late for that.

"The Number One rule, though, is that you can't, you shouldn't— I mean, it's just not a good idea to—book anyone because you're a fan. It colors your judgment, and you'll lose money every time, because you'll pay way too much just so that you can have *your* favorite artist in your room."

Well, shit. I had gotten myself into this business, and dragged my wife into this business and hoped to encourage my brother to dream in this business, because, first and foremost, I was a fan.

What now?

That's when it suddenly hit me that, without even realizing it, I had already slipped down that slope into the despairing dell of debt. No way that we could back out now. We had to make the most of this music thing, to dig out of our monumental obligations.

Now we could only sit and wait for him to drop yet another bomb or two, either on our immediate accomplishment or our immediate future . . . or both.

He smiled sadly and sighed. "Oh, and you won't make any money."

Despite his public persona that beamed a childlike ingenuousness, he had just annihilated our elation—mine, anyway. He must have sensed that, too, because he switched on a little pathos, and with a touch of compassion, he added: "That is to say, you might make a living, but you'll never get rich."

Oh, well, this whole enterprise was never about the money, anyway. I could always assuage myself with the knowledge that I was far too noble—and naïve and ignorant and had too much at stake financially now—to think otherwise.

The next day, the three of us dragged ourselves back to the mill. We felt like brand new college grads who suddenly understand that they'll never see summer vacation again. Somehow, amid all that ramping up for our Grand Opening, we started cobbling together a calendar. We would be open five days a week, Tuesday through Saturday, though we knew we would have to work on Mondays, and we would run from five p.m. until two a.m., except on Sundays; here in the very buckle of the Bible Belt, it was, at the time, anyway, forbidden to sell alcohol on the Sabbath, which began at midnight Saturday.

Early on, we did get some help with our calendar, a few shows here and there compliments of an "outside promoter," who also happened to be one of the most easily recognizable and certainly most recognized authority on music in town.

Before opening, we had met several times with Gene Berger, a lean, bespectacled and balding Greenvillian who bore a slight resemblance to one of his biggest rock 'n' roll heroes, Frank Zappa. Gene owned the local independent record store, Horizon Records, and was considered the "promoter of record" in the market. For years, he had booked major shows at the Peace Center, the elegant performing-arts theater downtown, where he had presented the likes of Emmylou, John Prine, Wynton Marsalis, Lyle Lovett and the Indigo Girls, among others. In our meetings, we hammered out an arrangement for Gene to book shows at The Handlebar, an opportunity he saw to keep his toes in the promotion ocean and a chance, if an unlikely one, to make a few extra bucks on the side.

As anxious as he was to start bringing big names to Greenville's small music scene, apart from his major concerts at the performing-arts center, Gene booked one of his favorite artists, David Lindley, the zany, self-proclaimed Prince of Polyester best known for his work with Jackson Browne. The trouble was that it soon became obvious that upfit construction on our space in the old mill wouldn't be anywhere near completed by the time Gene had contracted the show. So he had to move it somewhere else.

Unfazed, Gene contracted a guaranteed outta-the-park home run that would fall on the second night we were open: the red-hot New Orleans band, the subdudes. The band's third CD, *Annunciation*, was making waves nationwide, and even before The Handlebar's own Grand Opening, the buzz around town had grown as percussive as their own distinctive sound. Gene also booked an opening act for our next sold-out show, a little-known acoustic-blues musician named Kevin Moore, who went by his stage name, Keb' Mo'.

As if we needed any more stress after our Grand Opening the night before, that Saturday turned out to be riddled with glitches. For one thing, our room didn't have nearly enough PA to handle the sophisticated sounds of the subdudes—Gene had to rent a ton of additional gear—and, for another, we still had to get that damned piano off our stage in order to accommodate a band that could barely fit on it, anyway.

Still, three-hundred and fifty fans stood wall to wall in our sold-out house, and the lingering puddles of all the spilled beer reflected a much-needed cash boost that sent our hopes soaring.

We were making money; we could do this!

Then reality hit.

3

Unless you're Pete Seeger, Suzanne Vega or Emmylou, you've probably never heard of Rod MacDonald. Or maybe you didn't know that Rod has shared stages with those superstars. Or that he played a starring role in Greenwich Village's New Folk revival of the 1980s. Perhaps you're unfamiliar with Rod because you're just not a fan of folk music. Me, I'd grown up with folk music, a genre whose roots go back to the nineteenth-century coinage "folk lore," which has been defined as the "traditions, customs and superstitions of the uncultured classes."

I counted myself as one of Rod MacDonald's biggest fans. I'd seen him perform a few times in Florida and heard him on the radio in Tampa and even interviewed him for a novel I was writing during my carefree days as a fiction writer. I especially enjoyed Rod's smooth tenor and the social and political commentary that he packed into his melodies.

All of which helps explain why I had booked him to play the Monday after our Grand Opening weekend.

Of course, I had contracted his show long before Livingston Taylor issued his Number One Rule: Thou shalt not buy talent as a fan. Nevertheless, on that fuzzy October 3 afternoon, we were flying high, soaring with optimism after back-to-back sellouts.

Going into our first full week, we had what I believed to be a fairly decent concert calendar lined up for the next month or so. I had booked Patty Larkin, the New England chanteuse and monster guitar player and seriously funny chick; Steve Forbert, the charred-voice Mississippian whose "Romeo's Tune" had topped the charts a mere fourteen years before; and even a show for children, one of our early, clever attempts to market our new venue to adults.

Meanwhile, Gene Berger was busy working to appeal to *his* long-time, diehard customers. After the subdudes, he planned to promote: Webb Wilder, the self-styled "Last of the Full-Grown Men," whose work *Entertainment Weekly* called "Nashville's best country-on-peyote" Americana, whatever *that* was; and Freedy Johnston, the critically acclaimed "songwriter's songwriter" who peopled his songs with losers experiencing heartache and alienation—nothing says, *"Let's go party to some live music!"* like loners and letdowns.

But I was a fan of that stuff. And the night that Rod MacDonald arrived turned out to be my first colossal letdown.

That wasn't Rod's fault.

While we had been busy building our venue, the three of us still struggled to learn what we could about agents and artists and guarantees and offers, promotion and marketing. I knew as much about how *much* to offer a band or solo musician as I did about how to play guitar. All I knew was that strings were attached, you just needed to know how to tune them.

A month or so before we opened, I learned that Rod was coming through Greenville. He was looking for a gig, so I told him that we would guarantee him …a lot of money.

By the time he stepped on stage, things weren't looking good. Perhaps we hadn't promoted the show very well. Perhaps Rod and his music weren't widely known in our community. Or perhaps The Handlebar was just too new to have built the sort of following one can amass so much faster these days with the Internet and social media and Facebook and Twitter and…

When our sound guy dimmed the house lights, Kathy was there.

My brother and his wife, Melanie, sat in the front row. And I was there. That was it, the sum total of our crowd.

Thankfully, our company was flush with cash from the weekend's food-and-beverage receipts, such as they were. See, we had opened only with a beer-and-wine license from the state Department of Revenue's Alcohol Beverage Licensing division, in part because we couldn't afford the additional and costly liquor permit, but also because, purists that we were, we felt that all that booze would simply dilute the intimate live-music experience.

In any case, while the four of us enjoyed the intimate experience, and Rod graciously played a set as if the room actually had people in it, we girded ourselves for the worst.

That was when we learned one of the most critical components of the music industry—the whole thing about agents, which Livingston Taylor had tried to tell us about in his once-over-lightly tutorial. As it turned out, Rod didn't have an agent, fortunately for us; we had negotiated his contract directly with him. That meant that, unlike most artists who *do* have agency representation, he exercised total control, from his nightly appearance fee to his tour itinerary. Artists who have signed with agents don't have to worry about that stuff. Instead, an agent solicits the best offer from a promoter, who then signs a legally binding contract and returns it to the agency, along with the fifty-percent deposit. In other words, there may be no guarantees in life, but most of the music business is built on them.

Rod put down his guitar, asked for a beer and something to eat and told us to forget about our large, if wildly amateurish, guarantee. Instead, he said he would take only a few bucks for gas and a hotel room. He saved us from a painful loss, which not only turned out to be generous on his part but also astonishingly rare in a business where, I was learning quickly, the means of commerce had little to do with ends of art, where relationships supposedly built on music collapse under the weight of money.

I still keep up with Rod and his work.

⋮

Outside the mill, in what amounted to a non-existent personal life, Kathy and I began to settle in to Greenville. We lived in a two-story condo, about ten minutes from the office, close enough to get there in case of emergency; we knew that we would constantly face some kind of emergency. Meantime, we tried to navigate through the despair of debt and exhaustion and the fog of unfamiliarity with our new business and with our newly adopted hometown.

We discovered pretty quickly that Greenville itself had a long way to go in the trendsetting department. Not a single Thai or Vietnamese restaurant in sight, and only one or two cinemas offered first-run movies, no art-house theater. Downtown was all but boarded-up, save for a snazzy Hyatt and a cutting-edge café whose colorful Dutch owner, Addy, likely was as insane—and as lonely—as we were. Not long after we moved to town, the local arts-and-entertainment tabloid ran a "Best of the Upstate" poll. As the city's "Best International Restaurant," readers selected International House of Pancakes, which won the distinction three years in a row.

Yes, we were living the cliché, "You don't know what you've got 'til you've jettisoned it." We realized pretty quickly how spoiled we'd been in St. Pete: great food, year-round sunshine, beaches and tiki bars, well-paying jobs with regular, guaranteed paychecks, super benefits, lots of friends, swell places to go. On the bright side, we knew that we had ample opportunity to shake some hip into this hamlet.

But with our first real autumn in years adding a bite to the air, the real world, too, added a major bite of its own.

Precisely one week after the subdudes show, the morning of October 8 dawned clear and cold. The telephone rang in our condo. We knew few people here, so we had no idea who could be calling us so early; our family was well aware of our nocturnal schedule.

"You need to get to the mill," my brother said. "Immediately. Like, now."

In minutes, we raced over. We pulled into the back alley, to the rear entrance, so that we wouldn't have to walk down the long, dark, creepy hallway, where perhaps unsavory characters were still lurking.

Before we reached the double doors, we noticed several panes shattered in the bar-area windows. Someone apparently had thrown bricks through the glass.

In the turmoil preceding our Grand Opening, it hadn't occurred to us to install a burglar alarm. Besides, we had already burned through all of our working capital.

Inside, we traced a trail of busted shards and broken CD cases from the windows to the bar itself. Another trail led through the kitchen into the concert hall.

We flung open the door. Our soundboard was gone.

The eight-foot table that held our brand-new six-thousand-dollar console sat empty. It wasn't as if the equipment was heavy. Someone obviously had just picked it up and carried it out one of our two vulnerable and unchained concert-hall doors.

The soundboard, with its faders and dials and blinking lights and decibel meters, constituted not only a third of what we had spent on our entire PA, but it also was the very heart of our system. Without it, we couldn't put on a show.

That night, Patty Larkin was set to play.

In no time, though, Don, the tech whiz who had sold us our system and installed it for us, arranged to rent another console.

The show must go on.

Barely three weeks passed before we got another early morning call.

Since the first burglary, we still hadn't made the time or enough money to install an alarm system that would tie into the police and fire departments and summon authorities who, in a best-case scenario, would find only a false alarm and, worst-case, run off would-be thieves.

"Do you work at The Handlebar?" the caller asked.

"Who's this?" I already felt my heart sinking—*not again*? "Is there a problem?"

"I'm at Manifest Discs and Tapes, and we have a guy down here who's trying to sell us a stack of 'used' CDs." The independent record store, which was right around the corner from the mill, was Gene Berger's leading competitor at the time.

Oh, for crying out loud. I jumped out of bed, crushing the phone between my ear and shoulder, and started dressing for the inevitable race to the mill.

"The thing is, we noticed something strange about the tunes this guy brought in."

"Like what?"

He tried not to laugh; he was calling about what had clearly been a break-in at a sympathetic small business. "Well, the CDs that this guy wants to sell us, they're all . . . *folk music*. I mean, not to sound, y'know…but this guy—he's standing out at the counter right now—he doesn't look like the type who would, y'know, be into *folk music*. I would say that he's more into, I dunno, *urban*."

I was some pissed off now. All I wanted to do was drive straight to the record store and smack the living shit out of the thief.

"Okay, well, all right, but what really makes you think that stuff's ours?"

I heard *click-clicks* as he flipped through the jewel cases. "Let's see, we've got Mike Cross and Patty Larkin here, and as a matter of fact, the Patty Larkin CD even has an autographed ticket stub with it that says, 'The Handlebar.'"

"Well, hell!" I was anxious now to get to the mill and see what other devastation our latest burglar had wrought. "If you can, try to keep him there and call the police."

"I already did. I'm in our back office right now. I told the guy that I had to check on what we'd be willing to pay him for these CDs, in case we wanted to resell them, so he's still just waiting out front."

Kathy was already sitting up wide-eyed in bed. *Not again?*

I nodded.

That day, we scrounged up some money to install an alarm system.

But even before our first full month in operation was out, we saw the appeal of Being Your Own Boss and the glamour of show business all but vanish.

The relentless learning curve turned a rocky drive into a roller coaster ride. Among the myriad things we learned was what really goes into the price of a concert ticket. Fans don't generally know that when they spend their hard-earned coin to see their favorite rock star, they might also be paying for a well-greased goat or a pair of well-dressed hamsters.

Everyone knows the story of David Lee Roth and Van Halen's famous brown M&Ms. In a chocolate-covered nutshell: In 1982, Roth slipped the "brown M&Ms only" requirement into one of the band's "riders," the long and tedious "hospitality/catering" and "technical" addenda to the performance contract, which itself is often just a page or two and primarily details only the artist's guaranteed compensation, set times and so forth. But in its hospitality rider, Van Halen banned all *brown* M&Ms in its lengthy list of all the other stuff the band had to have backstage.

Roth later insisted that the demand wasn't capricious at all, but rather served as a test to see whether the promoters had paid sufficient attention to the other riders, namely the band's sophisticated technical requirements. If the promoters hadn't noticed the M&Ms proviso, he reasoned, they would also fail to stage the show properly—an oversight that could prove destructive, even life-threatening. Sure enough, when Van Halen pulled their semi-trailers into a Colorado venue, Diamond Dave, to his horror, found *brown* M&Ms mixed in with the others. Legally, that constituted a breach of contract. The band could have canceled the performance on that spot.

Legend has it that Roth went medieval on the dressing room

and caused twelve-thousand dollars in damage. The truth was that the staging *did* collapse under the weight of all that gear, resulting in eighty-five thousand dollars' worth of destruction.

From that moment on, Roth's rider, and its ensuing lore, launched a new tradition: pages of requirements with details that left every promoter wondering what was crucial and what was comic.

Right after we opened, perhaps because of the artists we present- ed or perhaps because of our size, we didn't see much of that non- sense. For the most part, we welcomed road-weary solo troubadours whose demands proved to be as low-key as they were. A favorite folkie, Vance Gilbert, would walk straight into our kitchen and raid our 'fridge, as casually as if he worked for us. Even Tish Hinojosa— yes! we booked Tish Hinojosa!—made herself at home, supping on our vegetarian chili and then asking for the recipe. Our performers mostly just wanted a hot meal and a cold beer.

Then came Leon Redbone.

In those days, the enigmatic Redbone had already been featured in *Rolling Stone* and had appeared on *Saturday Night Live*, which pro- pelled him to the Big Time. He was also beginning to make regular appearances on *The Tonight Show with Johnny Carson*. His marquee value was huge, and he was our biggest star to date.

Not only that, but his was the biggest guarantee we had ever offered, too, reflected in the cost of the highest-price ticket we had ever sold: twenty dollars. At the same time, his rider called for hun- dreds of dollars' worth of stuff—platters of specialty meats and exot- ic cheeses, candy, costly bottles of aged red wines, bottles of Jäger- meister and on and on.

My self-induced stress levels skyrocketed.

Stephen, meanwhile, handled all the grocery shopping.

Later, while my brother artfully laid out everything in the dress- ing room, he said, "Y'know, this is ridiculous."

"How long did it take you to gather up all this?"

"Man, this was more like a scavenger hunt. Do you know how

hard it was to find half the stuff he wanted in any of the stores around here?" He studied the table that was now groaning under so much "hospitality." "I mean, really, do you think it was necessary to get every single thing on the rider?"

"Of course, it is!" I said in my arrogant, patronizing naïveté; I had been the one who signed the contractually obligating contract and rider. "You *do* know that if Leon Redbone isn't happy with the catering and hospitality, he could up and cancel the show, just walk off." I had no idea if that was true, really. "And the show's sold out, so then what would we do?"

Soon enough, Mr. Redbone arrived for sound check. Only one other person traveled with him, his accompanist, a clarinet player. They had no band, no tour manager, just the two of them. They put their gear on the stage, then Mr. Redbone went into the dressing room. He surveyed the panoply of comestibles, licked his lips, picked up the bottle of Jagermeister and nodded in bewildered appreciation.

"What'd you go and get all this stuff for?" he asked in his goofy 1930s-era drawl. "There's only the two of us here tonight, we couldn't possibly go through all of this."

We wound up taking most of it home.

The next morning, Mr. Redbone called our office. "Say, did you happen to find my drinking glass?"

"Excuse me?" Kathy, asked. "Your—"

"Yes, yes, my drinking glass. It's my favorite drinking glass."

We went back to the dressing room and found a glass about as extraordinary as one you'd find in a motel bathroom.

She described the garden-variety water glass to him.

"Yes, that's it."

"Well," she said, "we have it right here. What would you like us—"

"That's delightful. You see, it's really important to me, so would you mind mailing it to . . ." He told us where to send his glass, which we packed with painstaking care and shipped, at our expense, to a venue where he would play several days later.

Otherwise, the night had gone well. The show sold out. We didn't lose any money, except perhaps on all that hospitality. For me, the relief was so great that I got as hammered as I'd ever been, drinking beer and expensive red wine with friends and with Mr. Redbone himself.

I quit drinking the next day.

After the Leon Redbone experience, we discovered a powerful tool in the music business: a black Magic Marker. With it, a promoter can legitimately and legally redact line after line, page after page, of "requirements" that ranged from truly important to downright impudent.

Our favorite rider came from a band called Silvertide. Silvertide had actually been booked as an opening band, but you wouldn't have believed that from their rock-star contract. In addition to the usual demands—bottles of liquor, beer, snacks, deli trays and whatnot— their hospitality list also listed the following:

> 2 6-Pack Hanes Crew Socks (Black or Grey)
> 2 Packs Cottonelle Flushable Baby Wipes
> 2 Live Hamsters in a Cage (one dressed like Indiana Jones, onedressed like a police officer—Hamsters to be returned.)

Another band, Sherwood, faced a similar Magic Marker treatment on its requests:

> 1 pack (6 pair) of Hanes black crew socks (size 6-12 or similar) [*What was with all these socks?*]
> 1 Greased Goat with Large Horns ← no skimping on this! We want that thing SLIPPERY!

Here's part of a real page from one Hospitality Rider:

Instruments – Artist's gear must be guarded by at least one hostile-looking, biggish guard who tells repellently boring stories.
Wardrobe – Nothing constricting or scratchy, except for Brock's thong.
Dressing Rooms / Backstage Area – Beginning two hours prior to performance, the backstage area must have a trophy delivered every ten minutes. Suggested trophies include "Most Beloved", "Best Show of the Year" etc. Creativity encouraged.

Additional Hospitality - <u>DO NOT</u> purchase any of these items until all buyouts and hospitality on page 9 have been addressed. H.A.N.D.

<u>**Knick Knacks / Food Extras**</u>
- One small package of Stroopwafels (Only if venue has hot coffee)
- Six-packs of any canned beverage for John to compare his abs to
- 1 Pre-1990 G.I. Joe Action Figure (W/Kung Fu Grip) still in package
- One sample packet of Aciphex
- One package of Gold Toe ankle high socks
- One Life-Size stand up cardboard Star Wars character (no Jar Jar)
- One 60s or 70s Jazz/Funk/Rock LP in NM condition (no Frampton)
- One package of black sharpies (gold & silver can be added to this)
- One Leatherman Skeletool Multi-Tool with nylon sheath
- One box of Trojan "Ultra Ribbed Ecstasy" condoms (Large Size)

Often, though, some riders offer clues to the artist's ego, while others include things that may seem silly but really are necessary to put on the show.

Songwriting hero John Hiatt asked for a fresh-roasted chicken, if only because he had endured too many curled-up deli-tray meats. Jazz icon David Sanborn asked for grilled salmon and steamed vegetables, if only because health issues required a macrobiotic diet. Bluegrass legend Del McCoury and his wife, Jean, and the boys asked for coffee and, maybe, some dessert, if only because they didn't want to inconvenience anyone. Likewise, avant-garde banjo stud Béla Fleck asked for nothing. And Chapel Hill's surf rockers Southern Culture on the Skids had to have a box of fried chicken, if only as a stage prop for their song, "Eight Piece Box"; the trio hurls the mess into the crowd. Their rider makes the demand clearly:

"NO CHICKEN = NO SHOW!!!"

Then you have the artist's technical rider. For the most part, the usually complex appendix concerns the house PA system and whether it will work for the band. Occasionally, a band will require

additional sound gear, and sometimes, the promoter must also provide backline, non-PA equipment such as a baby-grand piano, as
we had to rent for Livingston Taylor, or a drum kit or guitar amps,
because the band didn't travel with their own.

Aimee Mann was one of several who had to have an acoustic
piano hauled in, set up and tuned all at our expense; nothing says
pain in the ass on a rider like a baby grand. She also had to have hummus. We provided both, of course, even though she never touched
the hummus, and she had a fit about the piano, which, sadly, turned
out to be out of tune and had a sticky key.

Count that one a disaster.

Roger McGuinn, the Rock and Roll Hall of Fame inductee who
was lead singer, lead guitarist and a founding member of the Byrds,
needed a guitar amp and a particular microphone that helped dupli-
cate his trademark jingle-jangle sound. We finally found that one
specific mic, but the guy who owned it said he wouldn't rent the
fifteen-hundred-dollar piece to anyone, not even his wife. But it was
Roger McGuinn, we said, and the guy relented after we also gave him
tickets to the show.

Color that show just plain magic.

When The Roots played a private party at our place one Hallow-
een, all the band members and their tour manager flew in from New
York City, where they were the house band on a late-night network
television show. They brought with them only those instruments
that they could carry, so collecting and gathering the rest of the gear
they needed—drums, percussion, keyboards and the like—turned
out to be every bit as stressful and costly as any such scavenger hunt
before or since.

As we saw with The Roots, when you move up the celebrity food
chain and go from clubs to arenas, a few Magic Marker slashes just
aren't going to cut it. On a Website that reproduces celebrity riders, thesmokinggun.com, you find, for instance, that Jennifer Lopez
requires everything in her Green Room to be everything but green:

"white room, white flowers, white tables and/or tablecloths, white drapes, white candles, white couches. Yellow roses with red trim, white lilies, white roses." The Foo Fighters say they would be thrilled if the promoter provided "big-ass kielbasas that make a man self-conscious." These people aren't kidding. They have tour managers who enforce their contracts and riders, and even in the club business, some of them can make the experience trying, even disturbing.

Tour managers are almost exclusively men. They are generally large men with long hair, tattoos and chains linking their studded leather belts with their wallets. They arrive with voracious appetites, a burning need for coffee and the nearest john and an equally needy and often ornery crew of sound guys, guitar and drum techs and other roadies. Mostly, they are responsible for making their artists happy.

They are also enforcers, ensuring that their hosts each day, the promoters, adhere to the signed contract, and that riders are executed to their satisfaction.

Day by day and show after show, these guys tramped in: Panda, Fluffy, Stumpy, Wully and a *de rigueur* Tiny, who, of course, wasn't.

Some of them have been great, they made your day sail by.

For one memorable show, we all started the day knowing that we would lose *thousands* of dollars. I had offered the artist's agent a whopping eighteen-grand, more than we had ever guaranteed *any* artist. In the good-faith belief that we would sell out, despite the forty-dollar ticket, I was convinced—and, sadly, also convinced my presciently skeptical wife—that unloading a minimum of four-hundred and seventy-five tickets to cover just the artist's fee would be a no-brainer.

Not long after the show went on sale, the frightening dearth of sales warned us that our hoped-for revenues wouldn't materialize, that we would suffer a nearly irrecoverable beating.

The tour manager that day was named Phil. The seventy-five-year-old road veteran had seen everything anyone could see in this business, and then some. The most notorious Phil legend holds that in 1973 he stole the body of Gram Parsons, whose overdosed remains sat in a coffin on an LAX tarmac. Upholding a drunken promise he'd made to the country-rock pioneer, Phil and a friend borrowed a hearse, drove the body into the desert and buried Parsons. So when Phil showed up at The Handlebar, he already knew that we would lose enough money to buy a brand-new Kia—nothing big enough to transport a corpse maybe, but plenty enough to throw serious dead weight on our books.

Trying, then, to make the best of a dead-end deal, he walked into our place with a rubber chicken tied around his calf.

"Dude, what's with that thing on your leg?" one of our staffers asked.

"This?" he said. "My cock hangs below my knee."

Another night, another tour manager, Fabrizio, watched as his young charges stomped off stage, for no discernable reason, after playing for only twenty minutes. The crowd was pissed, and a clearly baffled Fabrizio was, too. As soon as he returned from the dressing room, where the band told him they wouldn't return to the stage, he handed me back all the money that we had just paid him for a show that had barely happened.

Some tour managers, on the other hand, seemed hell-bent on making our lives hell—presumably in the service of making their artists happy.

Take Brian, for example. He was the road manager for the Fabulous Thunderbirds, the seminal Texas blues-rock band whose hit song, "Tuff Enuff," still got occasional spins on our local classic-rock station.

The T-birds had already played The Handlebar once before, and Brian had made it clear that first time just how miserable he'd found the experience.

A year or so later, he called to advance the band's second—and final—show in our room. Tour managers typically call a promoter several weeks before the band's appearance to confirm details, iron out contractual obligations and ensure that all hospitality and technical requirements would be met. More important, they call to find out how and when they would get paid.

I happened to answer the phone when Brian called, and I immediately recognized his curt, clipped British accent.

"Oh, god," he said, "not you again."

" 'Scuse me?"

"I said, 'Oh, god, not The Handlebar again. I hate that room, I hate your PA, I hate your food. It was all so... detestable... last time.'"

Detestable. Nice. "Gee," I said, "we're just as delighted that you're coming back, especially since we lost money on you guys last time. But, hey, let's just go over the contract, shall we?"

So we did, but he still kept going: "Please explain to me, why *do* we have to come back to that dreadful place?"

"Beats me. I mean, I booked this show—unfortunately now, I see—because I thought maybe y'all would draw better this time, and we wouldn't lose money. But as for the other *whys*, hell, I don't know, you'll have to ask your agent. 'Course, you can always tell him not to make the same mistake again."

After Brian worked overtime to indulge his distaste for us the second time through, we then stereotyped all British tour managers as needy anal-retentive fussbudgets convinced that their jobs required the gravitas of a prison guard.

Another tour manager from Her Majesty's Empire proved that we weren't too far the mark.

This one turned out to be even more unusual, in that she was, yes, a woman.

Denise.

One beautiful May morning, Denise and her band's bus pulled in a couple of hours before lunchtime, for an atypically early load-in. As soon as she stepped off the tour coach, she looked around and sized up me and the four men who sat patiently by the side door. These guys were our loaders, strapping youngsters we had to hire, at our own additional cost, to move all the band's gear off the bus and trailer and onto our stage.

Denise crossed her arms and pursed her lips. "So. Where's the balance of our guarantee?"

"You're kidding me, right? It's ten o'clock in the morning." I looked at her chubby, imperious face in disbelief. "Your show's at eight-thirty tonight. We sent in the deposit a month ago." A demand for the balance of the band's guarantee had never hit me so early—or so hard. "Why would we have to… I mean, I just got here myself. We haven't even been to the bank yet."

We both paused before locking into a standoff, and we both looked at our loaders, who were barely awake and yet anxious to be done with their half-hour chore so that they could get on with their day.

Finally, I said, "How 'bout we just let these guys start loading in?"

"*Those* guys? Oh, believe me, nobody moves until we get paid. I have no intention of even *thinking* about unlocking the equipment trailer until you get us our cash."

I felt a competing desire to either throttle her or ask her one reasonable question: What if I were to pay her in full right now, and she simply up and left? Instead, I told her, "I can't do that."

"Then I won't unlock the trailer for your boys to unload anything. Not until I get paid."

"Y'know, while you stand here making such a ridiculous demand, you've already wasted money that's not in your contract on having my guys sit around doing nothing."

"Oh? It seems to me that you're the one doing the time- and money-wasting."

After I returned from the bank, things went downhill.

To Denise, *everything*, all day long, was wrong: the catering and hospitality, our menu; the stage, its dimensions and size; the PA; our loaders; the sound guy; our entire staff—none of it was quite up to her snuff.

She carried on through the afternoon, until I finally did something I had never done before: I called the band's agent to complain—and not just once, but five times.

"Who the hell is this chick?" I asked the agent. "She's batshit nuts and driving everyone here completely insane. You have *got* to get her out of my hair and out of everyone's face—or, at least, get her out of the building."

"Let me talk to her."

Nothing worked.

At 5:30 p.m., she still wasn't through with us.

"I don't really care what time you advertised the show to start," she said, "we're going on early. Plus, we don't like the way the chairs are set up, so if we don't start getting the things we want, we'll just cancel the show. Right here, right now."

After more than seven straight hours of her relentless abuse, I couldn't take it anymore. I pointed my finger in her face and screamed: "I swear to god! You say *one more word*, and I will call the police and have them haul your fat ass off my property ... *and* I'll have you ticketed for trespassing!"

She scurried back to the dressing room like a Chihuahua who'd just been nipped by a Rottweiler.

Thereafter, I was no longer allowed to deal with tour managers. Instead, our first line of defense would be our equable, indispensible administrative assistant and all-round go-to employee, Meredith. If anyone somehow managed to tangle with Meredith's unflappable efficiency, why, they would have to answer to Kathy.

So when another high-maintenance tour manager showed up, Kathy told me later, "Meredith and I decided early on that, from the very beginning and all day long, we would just look at him, smile and nod. Just smile and nod. He could yell at us all he wanted and make these crazy demands, but we would just smile and nod."

That didn't keep him from blasting them from beginning to end.

I would have lost it, but, Kathy said, "By the end of the night, the guy sat at the bar and had a few drinks. He carried on about how great everything was, how we'd made the day so 'easy' for him." By which time, Kathy said, she leaned over the bar and told him: " 'You know what? You're an ass. All day long, you never stopped complaining—about *everything*—and now you're sitting at *my* bar, after wrecking *everyone's* day, and you're telling me how happy you are?' The guy just looked at me." My wife rarely swears. "And then I told him, 'Go fuck yourself.' "

As if business, *any* business, the music business, isn't hard enough…

4

Years ago, before I lost enough of my mind to open a business that I knew nothing about, I was a swashbuckling, itinerant drunk who doubled as a newspaper reporter. Sometime back in that mist, Pulitzer Prize-winning columnist/diarist Anna Quindlen wrote a keeper line about journalism. Reporters, she said, step in and out of peoples' lives as easily as they do a pair of shoes. She thus nailed the best part of the job—never mind the steady, weekly, livable paycheck; the camaraderie of the newsroom and the besotted fellowship at the local bar after deadline; the byline; and the dreams of getting to a bigger paper that would take me to ever-more exotic places.

A lot happened along the way. Burnout, health issues, corporate politics, I left the newspaper racket.

So it was that I reached out to my brother to open The Handlebar.

As far as I was concerned, Stephen was stuck in a rut, and because he had saved my life with his kidney, I felt compelled to return the favor and help him with *our* dream, regardless of how ill-conceived that dream might be. After all, we had long toyed with the idea of our own music place, especially during our pilgrimages to McDibb's.

After I persuaded my soon-to-be wife to sign up for the operation and, in fact, manage it, operate it and do all the work, I plowed ahead doing what guys do best: I neglected the details.

For one thing, in planning this enterprise, it had never occurred to me that a nightclub would involve working mostly at night. That probably escaped my attention because I had spent a good part of my abbreviated career in newspapers on the evening shift. The second problem I overlooked in opening a service business was the part about service. In retail, you have to deal with people, namely customers and their money.

In the American newsroom—at least, the one that *used* to exist before the Digital Age—I was always surrounded by talented, educated wordsmiths who read and wrote for a living. My colleagues were innately curious and often ambitious, and their skills commonly matched their alcohol intake. In major metropolitan markets, in *those* days, anyway, newspapering was a contact sport.

But as a friend at *Time* magazine once told me, the reporters' game is played by young people with legs.

That was the rub—the grind, even. Not long after my transplant, the drugs I had to take to preclude my body from rejecting my brother's kidney started to work some unfortunate side effects. For reasons doctors still don't understand, those medicines, called immunosuppressives, cut off the blood supply to my hip bones, specifically, the balls that fit into the sockets, the femoral heads. Those joints started to erode, and when the cartilage in each died and disappeared, dying bone began grinding against bone. The pain was mind-bending and endless. Still, doctors at the time told me that I was too young for hip-replacement surgery. They said that, as a big-city reporter running around every day to get the story, I was too active. A prosthetic hip would fail in a snap, they said, and if that happened, the complications would be even more destructive. So, I had to live with the pain, they said, at least until I couldn't tolerate it anymore or until medical technology caught up with my inopportune youthfulness.

Stuck with all of that, I thought that I could simply run away from my problem. I soon abandoned my beloved career, which, coincidentally and perhaps because of my health, was going nowhere anyway. As soon as I left the newsroom, I also buried my own long-term dreams of becoming a foreign-correspondent or, at least, a "writer" or, even, an "artist."

So wouldn't you know? I went and created a business that demanded a lot of running around. Moreover, the physical, emotional and spiritual hits that chronically took a toll on me didn't do much to help with my, let's just say, *sociability*. In other words, I found that I wasn't all that good with customers.

Which turned out to be not such a great thing, considering that customers were the very people we needed to survive.

Oh, sure, I could be faintly charming every now and then. I had no trouble flirting with a pretty woman or engaging somebody I found fascinating in an entertaining conversation. But when it came to the faceless stranger or the amorphous mob, I could really blow it. In short, I learned that I simply wasn't wired for retail.

Small wonder that service industries post all those nifty, if cheesy, signs for their employees:

> *Happy faces make happy places.*
> *You have only one chance to make a good first impression.*
> *The best publicity is a satisfied customer.*

The only professional experience I had ever had with people outside the safety of the newsroom involved asking them questions for the day's story—and fleeing back to colleagues considerably smarter than I was. Until opening The Handlebar, I had never actually known a real "customer" before. To me, a "customer" was just some anonymous reader who called somebody in management to bitch about something he had read in the paper and claimed was wrong or inaccurate, and usually wasn't. At the same time, when I was a regular civilian outside the newsroom, I prided myself on being a low-maintenance patron in restaurants, bars and theaters. I was easily satisfied with whatever service I got from waiters and clerks who were just doing the best they could.

Thus I found myself as prepared for the retail side of our music business as I was to run a marathon.

Things seemed to go fairly easily for me during our Grand Opening—at least, as far as our service and our customers' satisfaction were concerned. Granted, nearly half of our fans that night included my parents, friends of my parents and similarly loyal well-wishers. The rest of the crowd seemed to include sympathetic supporters: curious and adventurous live-music aficionados who couldn't believe that Greenville now had a concert venue tailored to their tastes.

It also helped that Kathy had hired a great staff. Roger Martin was our bartender, an expansive, expressive Greenvillian who loved music and believed in what we did, and he could sell beer and wine as fast as anyone could order it. The bar was his stage, and Roger was a loud, funny, entertaining performer. On the floor, meanwhile, our new crew comprised smart and attractive students from nearby Furman University. Bright-eyed and energetic, the young people, Effie, Stacey and Ed, lit up the room.

As for me, well, I simply sat at my "new" recycled old metal office desk, our "box office." That first night, and for hundreds of nights afterward, all I did was sell tickets, take money and tear tickets. My dealings with actual fans generally lasted a few seconds. That turned out to be a good thing.

On our second night, after realizing with no small disappointment just how few concerts I would actually get to see as a music impresario, I managed to slip away just long enough to catch a bit of the show. Along the way, I also caught an earful from one of our new, all-powerful patrons.

After watching a few minutes of the subdudes' set, I stepped out for some fresh air. At the rear exit doors, I found myself face-to-face with a woman who had grudgingly left our smoke-free concert hall for a cigarette break.

Standing with a glass of white wine, she stopped me and asked if I happened to be one of the owners. Perhaps my handsome blue Polo shirt, with our new Handlebar logo stitched on the chest, gave me away.

"This sucks," she said.

Cue the sound of my giant internal balloon exploding. "What sucks?"

"This isn't at all what I expected."

"Oh?"

"Oh, yeah. See, I pictured this place to be set up like this: You came in, got great drinks at great prices and went straight into a show, where you got a table, some chairs, great food, personal service, a real, live concert hall where everything's cozy and comfortable. You sit, enjoy the show, drink, smoke…"

Was this chick insane? Had she ever even *been* to a rock club? Tonight wasn't your intimate, sit-down folk show, lady; no, that was *last* night, when Livingston Taylor played. Tonight, I'm afraid, featured New Orleans' funkiest, dancin'-est band this side of the Neville Brothers. Hadn't she ever been to Tipitina's or to the Maple Leaf, those storied Crescent City venues that were far more famous for their featured acts than their furniture?

"…this isn't at all what I thought I would be paying for," she went on. "Beer all over the floor. The place is packed. [*Bummer!*] No place to kick back, relax, enjoy the show. No tables in the so-called 'listening room.' [*With white tablecloths and flickering tea candles, too, right, à la some Bing Crosby supper club?*] And you can't even smoke where the music's playing? Seriously, you guys need to rethink a lot of things."

Not surprisingly, because this was only my second day on the job, all of this came as news to me—never mind that she actually even *said* all this stuff. I mean, whatever happened to our parents' mantra, which I presumed to be the same as most other parents' advice?: If you don't have anything nice to say, shut the hell up.

But wait just a second here, lady! How could you or *anyone* say anything negative about this place, especially after our Herculean efforts to open The Handlebar? We had just put everything we had into this business, and now you're saying that our brand-spanking-new, half-million-dollar investment was doomed.

I figured I had to take everything she said seriously. First of all, she might be speaking for everyone in the building and even all of her friends who may have heard about our place but hadn't quite got here yet. And, secondly, The Customer Is Always Right.

But, hold on …What *was* it, exactly, that she thought she was paying for that night? She had dropped only fifteen dollars on her ticket, and now she was telling me that she expected a first-class cabaret lounge? *For fifteen dollars?*

I also took her seriously because it just so happened that she was one of the state's most high-profile attorneys. Now, here she was, one of *my* customers! If she was unhappy with her experience, I thought, she might very well sue us. Soon enough, of course, I realized how ridiculous even *that* notion was. I further decided that some of her complaints sounded petty and, perhaps, might have been unfounded.

It didn't take much for me, then, to conclude that all the power that our capitalist system invests in The Customer was just plain bullshit.

Never mind that I now thought that the customer—shudder the idea!—was wrong, but he could also be a run-of-the-mill moron. Naturally, my freshly adopted attitude turned out to be impractical in our very-public business. Customers kept coming, and they appeared in all manner of shapes, sizes, ages, races, creeds, personality types and idiosyncrasies, with an endless variety of needs, expectations, hopes, wishes, demands, beliefs and baggage. Hell, they were just *people* being people. The trouble was that we faced thousands of them.

I just had to figure out how to handle the madding crowds.

Let's talk about the blues.

"Blues," Wikipedia says, "is the name given to both a musical form and a music genre that originated in African-American communities of primarily the Deep South of the United States at the end of the nineteenth century from spirituals, work songs, field hollers, shouts and chants, and rhymed simple narrative ballads."

In my opinion, blues also remains simultaneously one of the most misunderstood and yet one of the most easily recognizable *labels* in American music. Even rock 'n' roll, a term only coined in 1952, can mean just about anything, especially now, encompassing everything from indie to Goth metal. But blues is a different animal. A casual fan can ask, "Y'all got blues tonight?" and have some better-than-vague notion about what she wants and hopes to hear. (Same with bluegrass, but *those* fans are die-hards, many of them pickers themselves.)

And yet, to crib from Thoreau: Lots of folks profess to love music—in this case, blues—but "for the most part they give no evidence in their opinions and lives that they have heard it."

It was hard, if not impossible, to ignore the musical heritage of our erstwhile textile town, in a state that still flew the Confederate flag outside the Capitol building. South Carolina's Upstate was famous for the Southern rock of the Marshall Tucker Band; the pop-rock of Edwin McCain; the Piedmont blues of the Rev. Gary Davis and Pink Anderson; the beach music of The Swinging Medallions, who had influenced Bruce Springsteen; the smooth R&B of Peabo Bryson; the rockabilly of the Sparkletones; and the alt-country of Walter Hyatt and Champ Hood.

Through the '90s, though, it seemed that everyone wanted the blues. All over town, people said they were hungry for blues—if only because, perhaps, it's the musical equivalent of a hamburger: You have an instant, mouth-watering image of what you want.

But I soon learned that, with blues, what you think you're going to get may not be what you see.

The great British blues/rock pioneer, John Mayall, summed it all up when he played his first Handlebar show. He brought with him an ace guitar slinger, Buddy Whittington, who carried on Mayall's legacy of hiring the world's best guitar players. Mayall had started performing in 1956, and his band, The Bluesbreakers, went on to jumpstart the careers of Eric Clapton; John McVie and Mick Fleetwood, both of Fleetwood Mac; Mick Taylor, later of the Rolling Stones; Walter Trout; and the left-handed Coco Montoya.

Before he took our stage the first time, Mayall told me: "Blues is dangerous music played by dangerous people for dangerous fans."

At the same time, I had to wonder, while I listened to Mayall's keyboard- and guitar-driven rock, was this *really* blues? Didn't matter. Mayall called his music blues, and fans called it blues, and because that brand of blues packed our room with blues-loving fans, why, blues would be the ticket for us to make a little money.

Or so I thought.

Hoping to cash in on the market's apparent craving for blues, I booked some of the country's best-known blues performers: Koko Taylor, Junior Wells, Lonnie Brooks, the Fabulous Thunderbirds, Carey Bell, James Cotton, Drink Small and even the acoustic blues of Roy Book Binder and John Hammond Jr., whose father, incidentally, had discovered Bruce Springsteen. I booked the region's own blues bands, too: the ribald Nappy Brown; keyboard hero and vocalist Skeeter Brandon; Cootie Stark, Greenville's own version of Robert Johnson; and area blues-rockers True Blues, Electric City Blues Band, Mack McCloud and the Hipshakers; and more.

We lost money on too many of those big names.

Then we promoted Tinsley Ellis. The first night he played our room and for many nights thereafter, the Atlanta guitar slasher incinerated the place, giving 'em what they *really* wanted: fiery Southern rock with a blues inflection. While fans insisted that Tinsley played kickass blues, his sound was informed more by Lynyrd Skynyrd than Stevie Ray Vaughan. Even Tinsley would tell you that he was a rock 'n' roll musician whose pyrotechnical licks included some blues influences.

Of all the nights that we presented the blues, Junior Wells had to be the wildest and most fun—and, for me, the most frustrating.

When he arrived in Greenville in September 1996, Amos Wells

Blakemore Jr. was an old man, though not in terms of age, but in terms of how hard he'd been rode. The night I met him, Junior Wells wore a garish, canary-yellow leisure suit, a style that had gone out of fashion in the 1970s, back when he jammed with the Rolling Stones and Buddy Guy. He also sported one of those cheap mesh cowboy hats, also neon yellow, but grimy and smushed and old.

Junior Wells and I sat on a bench out near the bar while his band was assembling just down the ramp in our concert hall. The stage barely accommodated all ten of his musicians, but they somehow squeezed together. He slumped next to me and, with his long bony hands, fingered one of his harmonicas and a microphone; our PA had been designed so that a performer with a wireless mic or wireless guitar could play out in the bar while everyone could hear the music in both rooms. Tinsley had done that a few times, even walking outside the mill and shredding all the while, as fans listened to him play and wondered where he'd gone.

So here I was, sitting next to one of Chicago's gen-u-wine old-school legends, the "Hoodoo Blues Man" who had also played with Van Morrison, Bonnie Raitt and Muddy Waters.

"How ya feelin', Mr. Wells? Can I get you anything? Do you need anything before you go on—water, beer, food…?"

"Oh, no." He shook his head, then leaned over and whispered, "I …am one…old… muthafucka."

He chuckled and wobbled to his feet. Two comely women appeared and linked their arms with his and accompanied his shuffle down the ramp toward the concert hall.

Then he brought his harp to his lips. And he began to blow.

Only about a hundred and eighty people were waiting to see him in a room that could have—and should have—been packed with three hundred or more of all those fans out there who'd been screaming for the "blues."

When he finally walked in, still wailing on his harmonica, he parted the crowd like some biblical sea. The band exploded. The fans went wild.

We lost money on the show, too. Junior Wells never returned. The evening that he played for us, he was sixteen months away from dying at the age of sixty-three.

One night, after a flurry of blues shows that just couldn't pull in the fans the way the harder electric blues-rockers could, we got a call from one of our new, sometime regulars.

When I answered the phone, I was delighted to hear from John, a supportive patron who was also a brilliant businessman. He worked in the financial-services industry, he was smart and well-connected, and we occasionally turned to him for advice.

"Do you all have a band tonight?"

Yes, John, we have a band tonight. It's what we do. You might as well call a movie theater and ask if they show movies. But I didn't actually say any of that. "Uh. Yeah. We've got a band."

"What kind? I'm a big blues fan," he said.

Oh, right, of course. Like everyone else around town. Okay, sure. Despite our recent spate of blues shows—authentic, hard-core, legendary, Grammy Award-winning blues—he and his wife hadn't attended a single one of them.

"Blues? As a matter of fact, I'm happy to say that tonight, yes, we do have a blues band. But…" I couldn't help pushing my point with some obnoxious, smart-ass snark. "Geez, I don't know, what *kind* of blues do you like? Electric blues, acoustic blues, jump blues, swing blues, roadhouse blues, old blues, new blues, Chicago blues, Piedmont blues, Delta blues, Texas blues, swamp blues—"

"Well, no, I…"

Oh, for crying out loud, *blues is blues*! You want blues and you're a blues fan? Who cares what *kind* of blues it is? *If you want to hear some blues, come hear some freakin' blues!*

John never returned to our establishment.

Still, we continued booking great blues bands. Sometimes those shows worked, but never as much as we wanted them to, and often those failures ended up to be just as baffling as they were maddening.

For instance, Kathy and I managed to get away from work one night for something of a busman's holiday. Bonnie Raitt and her band were playing Greenville's elegant and acoustically perfect performing-arts theater, the Peace Center. We paid forty-five dollars a ticket, but we'd also pulled a string or two to snag front-row seats. I had never seen the goddess of American roots-blues, so I was ecstatic.

But first we were treated to her opening band, Jon Cleary and The Absolute Monster Gentlemen.

Jon, who also played keyboards for Bonnie Raitt, warmed up the show with a set unlike any I'd heard since the Neville Brothers, the subdudes, Dr. John or Marcia Ball, the chief exporters of Louisiana's signature gumbo rock. Jon and his boys were tight and bouncy, jumpin' through greasy, rollicking Crescent City blues, as much fun as it was infectious.

Halfway through their allotted forty-five minutes, I turned to look around the hall. The auditorium was all but empty. Only a few hundred of the sold-out, twenty-one hundred seats were occupied. Everyone else remained in the lobby, rubbing shoulders and cocktailing and waiting for the headliner. They were missing this opening act! (Which, apparently, is the preferred and conventional way to spend the first forty-five minutes of your forty-five-dollar ticket.).

Meanwhile, I couldn't get enough of Jon Cleary and His Absolute Monster Gentlemen. His guitar player alone was worth the price of admission, a ginormous African-American man whose girth made his guitar look like a ukulele and whose smile was every bit as big.

As soon as I got back to the office, I booked the band.

Six weeks later, only a handful of patrons showed up. Nobody, essentially, had seen Jon Cleary and his band at the Peace Center. Anybody else who *hadn't* attended the show had no idea who they were.

Still, we did see the casual blues fan who actually did show up for a blues show just because it was a blues show.

On a dreadfully slow night that featured a top-notch local outfit, Electric City Blues Band, I was sitting morosely at my desk alongside my brother. Stephen was commiserating with me about all these ill-fated blues shows when we looked up to see a large man loping toward the ticket desk.

His ball cap was pulled down over his eyes. He wore a nondescript windbreaker. He looked faintly familiar.

"Hey," Stephen whispered. "You know who that is?"

I shook my head.

He could barely contain himself before the outsized patron walked up. "That's Dan Aykroyd!"

"That's no more Dan Aykroyd than I am Jake Blues."

"Just wait…"

I gazed up at the man's shaded face. He dropped a ten-dollar bill on the desk. I reached into the drawer for his change, while Stephen handed him his ticket.

"But, sir," I said, "the admission tonight's only five bucks."

"Keep it. Give it to the band."

Apparently, the Blues Brothers star was filming a movie in North Carolina and had heard that a blues band was in town. He wanted to check out Electric City, perhaps to play their music on his House of Blues radio show.

In the back of the dark, sparsely populated room, he waved away our one attempt to give him a bottle of water. He sat by himself and tapped his feet to the rhythm of the blues.

As time ground on, business grew, thankfully, but our ever-expanding demographic became, at least for me, that much more exasperating, amusing, interesting, infuriating, annoying and even loveable.

Businesses evolve and adapt, especially those trading in popular culture, which itself shifts like the time signatures in a Rush or Tool tune. I continued seeking different varieties of music, much of which had never or rarely been promoted in the Upstate. At the same time, I also tried to respond to the warp and woof of the industry in general and to the peculiarities and demands of our market in particular. Fads may change, but fans often didn't—we just needed to get more of them.

So I ventured beyond our original, if limited, folk-music offerings. We promoted more and more bluegrass and its spinoffs, more and heavier rock, metal and punk, and reggae and world music, even getting into Zydeco and, one time, the klezmer band that had played Lyle Lovett and Julia Roberts' wedding. And after Jerry Garcia's death in 1995, when the Grateful Dead gave way to Phish and Widespread Panic and the proliferation of jam bands, we got into those, too. I booked, among others, Leftover Salmon; Dirty Dozen Brass Band; Jupiter Coyote, from nearby Brevard, North Carolina; and Sound Tribe Sector 9, before their electronica-dub sound and before renaming themselves STS9—in fact, one of their earliest CDs includes a bonus track recorded live at the old mill.

The jam-band shows drew hippies and neo-hippies, the Trustafarians and tie-dyed yuppies who became our most loyal and enduring fans and often our most endearing and amusing ones. They danced and twirled in their batik skirts and multihued professional-cook's pajamas, swaying and swirling to endless tunes that drew heavily from bluegrass, jazz and rock. In something akin to evangelical ecstasy, they waved their arms, as if reaching for Jerry or swatting at the lingering notes.

One night at a sold-out jam-band show, a patchouli-flavored woman wandered in cradling her newborn. She had the wistful, distant look of a stoned Pietà. Her voice carried that telltale bong-seared purr.

"Is it okay if I bring her in to the show?" she asked.

"Sure!" We had always made our Age Policy clear: Anyone younger than eighteen was welcome, but *only* with a *parent*. We had long since decided that anyone old enough to vote or go off and shoot foreign combatants was also eligible to buy a ticket; we just couldn't be responsible for minors. In this case, though, I wondered why any parent would want to accompany her unconscious infant to a rock concert.

She appeared delighted with my answer. "Cool! See, in, like, two weeks, she and I, we're going on the road with the Dead"—what remained of them, anyway—"and this is, like, really good practice for her."

Right on.

One morning, our office assistant, Vince, answered the phone with the typical expectation that he would field a garden-variety question or ticket order or random booking call. Instead, a young man was on the other end, his gravelly vocal chords roasted and his synapses clearly fried.

Later, when he recounted their conversation, Vince mimicked the young man's elongated words, the slow speech that curled out and lingered like so much aromatic smoke.

"Dude…I called, uh, because I was just, uh, wondering…"

"Yeah?" Vince asked.

The young man coughed a little, perhaps in mid-inhale. "Oh, yeah, uhhh, see, I was, like, there, at the show…?" Long pause. Many of these kids spoke in sentences that ended in ellipses or question marks—you could hear the punctuation.

"Ohhhh-'kay," Vince said.

"Yeah, and, dude, do you have, like, a Lost and Found?"

"Just like a Lost and Found, sure, but it's all just in this little jar that we keep in the office … Sorry, yes, what did you lose? We can probably find it around here somewhere and get it back to you."

"Well, okay, I was at the show last night? And … have you seen my pants?"

Over time, other fans would turn out not to be fans at all, but mere curiosity-seekers who may have heard their friends mention that The Handlebar offered entertainment. Those were the people whose questions reflected not only their own multiplying diversity but the increasing variety in our monthly calendar.

It had always seemed to me that most folks don't customarily call, let's say, an Italian restaurant and ask about the freshness of the day's fettuccine or just how "al dente" the noodles would be cooked. Likewise, most bluegrass and jam-band aficionados knew what they were buying.

But rock fans are a different story, especially the classic-rock ones. And with classic rock becoming that much more "classic," which is to say that fewer and fewer rock 'n' roll dinosaurs still wandered the jungles of Clubland, the touring business found the Next Big Thing: tribute bands. So we booked a Doors tribute band, a Journey tribute band, KISS Army, The Dave Matthews Tribute Band and, our most popular tribute band, ZOSO: The Ultimate Led Zeppelin Experience, though one could argue that the "ultimate Led Zeppelin experience" would have been to see the original item.

Obviously, most fans knew what they were getting when they bought a ticket to one of these shows, but that didn't keep the questions from coming.

One woman asked: "What kind of music does the Dave Matthews Tribute Band play?"

Another patron walked out of the concert hall in a swoon: "ZOSO kicks ass! Where can I get their CDs?"

Too often and at times spectacularly, I failed in my less-than-halfhearted attempt to indulge some of our customers their often-delightful and sometimes-incomprehensible ignorance. Fortunately, some of their questions just didn't have answers, so I didn't have to supply any:

"Y'all got the balls to charge money for live music?"

"Are you a black club?"

"Are you a gay club?"

"Is the food there any good?"

"Do you have to pay to eat?"

"How do you eat here?"

"What's 'will call?' "

"You people say you're a music place, so why don't you have karaoke?"

Every now and then, a fan just wants to game the system. Our Age Policy is a favorite target:

"I was just wondering, if you buy tickets in advance for a show, do you still need to be eighteen to be admitted?" And the instant classic:

"How old do your parents have to be?"

Then there are the times that my failure to bite my tongue would bite me in the ass.

One night, a potential customer walked in and asked me straight-away: "Is the band you got here tonight any good?"

I might not have tried as hard as I could have to hold back. I mean, I was pretty proud of our lineup—you know, *having booked it.* "No," I said, "in fact, these guys suck. Which is why we booked them. We just thought…"

She gave me the finger.

The worst part, though: my inappropriate elitism and unfounded arrogance have occasionally infected some of our employees, who get paid to respect, nurture and win the enduring loyalty of each and every customer.

A woman walks into a bar… stop me if you've heard this one.

She was apparently lost in the building, though not by much because our building's just not that big, and the bar area, the front half, has windows. At any rate, she stood just around the corner from the main entrance, near the windows that were still framed in daylight. When our longtime bartender, Heather, happened by, the woman stopped her and asked, "Where's outside?"

Heather pointed toward the door and through the windows. "Outside? It's right there, just like inside, only big and pretty."

Heather, a word of advice: My wife has fired me several times, from my own company, for doing stuff like that. But, really, I get it.

The day-to-day crises and routine pettiness of small business, retail and the music industry may conspire to drive some people—me, for instance—insane. But when larger circumstances, totally out of your control, seem determined to wreck your entire livelihood, you can lose more than your mind. You can lose *everything*.

5

As early as 1997, we began to feel ominous rumblings in the old mill. Not from construction or its long-hoped-for renaissance; no, we would never be that fortunate. Instead, the old physician and his partners sold the building to a solo operator, a man we'll call "Jud."

It was said that Jud had purchased the building for $1.2 million. It was said that he had paid $850,000 of that in cash, with the balance financed by the doctor, who, as it turned out, wasn't much longer for this world. At least one document listed the official transaction price as "one dollar."

Those tidbits were just a *soupçon* of the lore that enshrouded the mill's new owner, our new landlord.

As far as we could tell, Jud was little more than a garden-variety strip-club owner. But some insisted that he was a genius. Legend around town had it that he had graduated from M.I.T. He owned several businesses, primarily nudie bars and dive bars, all stocked with video-poker machines, the state's form of legalized gambling at the time. Before South Carolina abolished the three-billion-dollar-a-year industry in 2000, the machines fed Jud's conspicuous hunger for cash.

He purchased the old mill in 1997, and from Day One, he proceeded to make our lives hell.

At first glance, he seemed to be merely a menace. Whenever we saw him, he barely made eye contact. He simply shuffled through the dark hallways, always whispering into his cell phone. From time to time, he muttered at us through a grim smirk that made you think he'd just as soon shoot you, even though most folks doubted that he believed in that sort of thing. He almost always carried a sixteen-ounce Styrofoam cup, and despite his gray-white hair, his age seemed as indeterminate as everything else about him.

Few people seemed to actually know the man or much about him. Some claimed that he had the gift of Midas and the treasures—hidden, buried or laundered—of Croesus. One myth said that he had made his initial fortune this way: When bulky personal computers gave way to laptops and desktops with microprocessors, he cannibalized the clunkers for their gold solders.

While he indeed may have kick-started his fortune with gold flakes, he amassed the bulk of it from bars that sold cheap booze and cheap thrills, not to mention a stream of cash that flowed from all of those then-legal video-poker machines.

Those were also the days of mini-bottles, the little 1.7-ounce shots of liquor that every alcohol retailer was required to sell; all those silly little bottles made South Carolina look like one massive airliner, but they certainly made for stiff drinks, too. They also earned the state a stiff fortune; taxes reached as high as forty cents per bottle, drastically cutting into retailers' profit margins. Jud solved that problem. He simply bought up mini-bottle cases by the palette to leverage his near-wholesale volume throughout his retail empire.

Jud's primary form of transportation was a Chevy van with Venetian blinds that covered the windows. Some days, though, he pulled up in the mill's back alley in an El Dorado or Gran Torino. Some folks said that he frequently drove one of those beaters down to Mexico, its trunk loaded with cash. No telling what he did down there, but a

Greenville cop once regaled me with stories that made my authorial imagination concoct a couple of blockbuster screenplays.

Jud was married to a voluptuous sexpot, a Mexican who appeared to be about half his age. Stiletto heels and skimpy outfits showed off her *Playboy* physique, which belied no obvious signs that she had produced a *mestizo* or two; Jud occasionally carried the children through the hallways. She apparently ran her own businesses, including one, mostly in absentia—a ridiculous little import/export shop in a space on the mill's second floor. The store was rarely, if ever, open, and was filled with the same brightly colored *tchotchkes* that you'd find in a fleabag border town: flimsy marionettes and outsized *sombreros*, obnoxious *maracas* and plaster of Paris statues of Felix the Cat and ET.

On the first floor, Jud soon started work on a "classy" restaurant, spending thousands of dollars in renovation, including fancy and costly Saltillo tile throughout the shiny, fully equipped kitchen. The end result was a seafood joint as dark and foreboding as the food was bland and inauthentic. In the bar sat two video-poker machines, where the occasional mope would slide in a dollar a play for the fat chance to win a slim dream.

Jud made it clear from the get-go that his designs never included us. Never mind that we were growing a business that drew increasingly more patrons into his all-but-empty mill. He simply didn't like us. He also didn't like the fact that his restaurant was bombing and that our customers wouldn't eat there. One of his lawyers—the very same woman, as it happened, who had told me of her disappointments during the subdudes show—said that he found us elitist, snobby and arrogant. Which we were, if only because we had earned some of our pride by running a solid, above-board, high-integrity operation—without the benefit of video-poker machines.

As much as all that, too, he evidently had no clue what our business actually did.

One night during a sold-out show with John Mayall & the Bluesbreakers, I swallowed what I could of my contempt for the man when I saw him walk through the mill's back doors.

I approached him and tugged on his crumpled white Oxford shirt.

"Jud! You gotta see this!"

I led him down the ramp and into the packed concert hall. The joint was jumpin' and vibrant, with Mayall and his band bursting at the buttons. One couldn't help but be enthralled with the keyboard-pounding Briton whose influence still reigned over blues and rock. Jud just stood in the back of the room, against the sound booth. He crossed his arms. For the next ten minutes, he didn't move. He occasionally nodded his head. His feet didn't tap or twitch. His fingers didn't, either. The man clearly had no idea that he was witnessing a legend.

Soon, he brushed by me and walked out, muttering, "Guy's pretty good."

Guy's... pretty... good? Seriously?

Each passing month brought another broadside from the inscrutable landlord, who kept ratcheting up the tension with letters and notices that cajoled and threatened, aimed at driving us out before our lease expired; we had already renewed our agreement with the previous landlord. For instance, even before Jud moved in, we had tried to keep the mill's big and unkempt parking lot tidy, but Jud and his smarmy real estate representative warned us: If we find so much as one cigarette butt out there, you lose your lease. Next, they threatened to seal off the entire mill—that is, they would lock the building's front entrance at six o'clock every night, ostensibly to prevent random trespassers from wandering around the other, vacant floors. At the same time, we would be required to lock our end of the mill, the double doors at the rear entrance, close to our bar.

In one of my several finely tuned epistolary responses, I informed Jud and his lackey that their proposed lockdown would violate City

Fire codes, though I didn't mention that I also considered reporting their evil scheme to the ever-vigilant Mr. Cook, the fire marshal. My letter went on:

> Do you wish to make it appear to our customers—both by the locking of the doors and the fact that no lobby lights currently work—that The Handlebar is closed? Do you wish to make access to The Handlebar inconvenient to our customers? What exactly do you mean when you suggest that The Handlebar "negotiate" for access with (your representative); we believe that legal and safe access is an implied guarantee of any lease.
>
> Without further explanation of these issues from (you), The Handlebar can only assume that your letter…is simply another form of the harassment that we have experienced since (your) purchase of Mills Centre.

We received no response to that.

Still, their half-witted intimidation continued, until they came up with their best threat yet. In one of his last attempts to boot us from his building, Jud complained that The Handlebar was consuming too much water and that the mill's incomprehensibly high water bill stemmed from our…ice machine.

Having once been a professional reporter, I did a little pre-Google research. I looked at the specifications of our particular machine. The contraption could make and hold five hundred pounds of ice. According to Jud, The Handlebar consumed *seven* full loads every week. If we really went through that much ice, give or take a few hundred cubes, I calculated that we would have to be serving as many as eleven-thousand highballs every week. (By that time, incidentally, we had finally gotten a mini-bottle license, to start making actual money.) That's one hell of a lot of drinks to sell in five days, with only three shows on average. Taking the average price of our mixed drinks and applying that to Jud's numbers, his figures could mean only one of two things: Either our customers, who numbered fewer than three hundred each week, were getting spectacularly hammered, or we just couldn't account for nearly fifty-grand in weekly liquor receipts. The bottom line was that if Jud's math were correct, we would be banking two-hundred-thousand dollars a month *just off cocktails*. And if *that* were true, why, I would have already bought the mill, along with an island in the Caribbean.

Never mind that we didn't have time to deal with all this hectoring, but I finally pointed out that our lease stated that the landlord was responsible for paying the water bill—regardless of how high it was or how it got that way.

Still, he would hear nothing of it. We either shut off our machine, or, par for his course, we faced eviction.

Eventually, though, he caved.

Still, he kept tightening his screws. Obviously, the mill just wasn't big enough for both of us.

The century, meanwhile, played toward its finale. Along with the global freak-out over Y2K, while the record industry hovered on the verge of digital meltdown, we also faced a future as uncertain as Robinson Crusoe's. Yes, we still lived with more debt than cash, sort of like the government. And while most everyone agrees that money doesn't buy happiness, it does buy memories. Lots of them. We collected and stored them up like so much cordwood to keep us warm whenever the big cold world got that much colder.

As it always has been and always would be, the music endured.

Among the hundreds of shows that we had presented, a handful come to mind: Nils Lofgren, Mickey Newbury and Gillian Welch with David Rawlings. (Other fans might disagree; any list of favorite Handlebar concerts would be as subjective as every *Rolling Stone* Greatest Album, Greatest Guitar Player, Greatest Rock Song.) But those three shows in particular, and in memory, all pulled me into the Listening Room, where I watched in admiration and wonder, every moment suspended in time.

It was amazing to me that we could even book Nils Lofgren. He had once belonged to Neil Young's Crazy Horse, but was perhaps best known for his acrobatics in Springsteen's E Street Band, where he would flip on a trampoline while he played. (In 2011, *Rolling Stone* named him the fourth Greatest Guitarist of All Time, between Jimmy Page and Jeff Beck.)

In February 1996, the diminutive performer showed up with a hirsute band of grouchy roadies and some of the most amazing musicians in the business. It's pretty hard to keep track of the hundreds, even thousands, of band members who come through, but Nils had hired some serious sidemen: on guitar and keyboards, Jeff Thall, who had played with John Cale and Bryan Ferry; on bass and vocals, Wornell Jones, who had worked with the Pointer Sisters and Earth Wind & Fire; and Andy Newmark, a drummer for damn near everybody, from Cat Stevens to George Harrison and Sting to George Benson. Andy had appeared on Carly Simon's 1971 album, *Anticipation*, and was the sole drummer on John Lennon's last album, *Double Fantasy*. To say that Nils's band that night was among the best group of musicians we had ever seen would be like saying that Shakespeare wrote good.

The quartet packed those hundred minutes with long, elegant jams and jaw-dropping guitar wizardry that skirted the line between rock and jazz. He spoke little to the crowd, which filled only about half the room, stopping only once to comment on the meager size of our stage:

"Kinda tight up here," he said. "I think you've got a lot more room than us, but this way we can't hide anything from you. That's all right." He chuckled. "No, this is nice. It's like my basement, except there's a lot more people, and instead of feeling like work, this is fun."

Once again, too many people missed that show, but those who did see it, I knew, would remember it forever.

Likewise, Mickey Newbury played two shows in the years before emphysema killed him in 2002.

Waylon Jennings and Willie Nelson had immortalized Mickey in their song, "Luckenbach, Texas," with the lyrics, "Newbury's train songs." Elvis had turned Mickey's "American Trilogy" into a concert staple and showstopper, while Mickey's "Just Dropped In (To See What Condition My Condition Was In)" was Kenny Rogers's first Top Ten hit.

Mickey's voice was liquid silver and his guitar work tasty without being flashy. His songs defied categorization, with writing that recalled Stephen Foster—Mickey was a huge fan—and James Dickey.

South Carolina native Jack Williams had pulled Mickey back out on the road. An accomplished guitarist and songwriter in his own right, Jack had played with, among others, Harry Nilsson and John Lee Hooker. During their shows, he sat next to Mickey and played his acoustic guitar with restraint that whispered along in harmony.

Mickey performed for small audiences both times, his debut concert at The Handlebar's first anniversary and again in November 1997. On stage, he chatted amiably with Jack and the crowd, telling lighthearted tales, often laced with comments about the business that had always underappreciated and underpaid him in a life that he apparently had no other choice but to live.

"Being a songwriter's a hard ol' deal," he said in his last appearance for us, "and yet you're the luckiest person in the world if you can do what you love to do and make even a good living at it."

Earlier, in the dressing room, he had cradled his hard-body wood guitar, stained dark, with intricate carvings. Chet Atkins had given it to him, he said. When I asked him if he needed anything and asked how he was doing, he told me about the agony that would eventually kill him. But he said, "When I begin to sing, all the pain goes away."

I peered out to the smattering of fans, who were bubbling over with anticipation.

"They look and sound like they're out of control," I said.

"Johnny boy," he said, his sky-blue eyes twinkling, "that's my concern, nothin' you have to worry about. Y'see, that's my job. Any performer who can't control his crowd, can't bring 'em around to where he wants 'em, he isn't good enough to be out on that stage."

That night, you could almost hear the flutter of an angel's wings.

During another enchanting evening, you could swear that crickets were singing along.

Before Gillian Welch and David Rawlings took the stage, somebody out in the neighborhood somewhere had dropped a backhoe on a power line, killing all the electricity in the building. The two still agreed to play, despite the absence of a PA system.

Gil had been known for her homely print dresses and a voice and songs that evoked some deep Appalachian holler, while Dave played with technical prowess that fused the best of bluegrass and the best of rock. Together, the two sounded like one.

Only our battery-powered emergency lights and the golden glow of a parking lot lamp just outside the concert hall windows cast an otherworldly radiance on the room. You'd have thought that you were transported to the back porch of some cabin in 1930s Kentucky, listening to a transistor radio and nature's nocturnal symphony.

Other noteworthy shows included Eddie From Ohio's performance with Mark O'Connor, Maynard Ferguson's surreal concerts and the once-in-a-lifetime Béla Fleck appearance.

One night, our friend Gene Berger was promoting a show at the Peace Center with the genre-exploding violinist/fiddler Mark O'Connor, and in the afternoon, he had invited Eddie From Ohio to play a brief in-store set to help promote their Handlebar show. While EFO was at Horizon Records, they met Mark, whom Gene brought to the mill before his own Peace Center gig. Mark typically carried his costly instrument with him wherever he went, and when he stepped backstage to chat up EFO, they invited him onstage for a song or two. Here was an internationally renowned Grammy Award winner who just whipped out his fiddle and jammed through a couple of unfamiliar tunes.

"How does he know their songs?" Kathy asked.

"He doesn't," I guessed, "he's just playing by ear."

The crowd went wild. They had no idea what hit 'em.

Likewise, I was blown away when Maynard Ferguson and his big band turned a jazz show into a rock show. Maynard brought his trumpet to his lips, puffed his cheeks like water balloons and sent notes into the stratosphere. He and his band played everything from "The Girl From Ipanema" to his mainstream hit, "Gonna Fly Now," from *Rocky*. Equally remarkable was Maynard's generosity. Throughout the show, he stepped aside to let his super-talented charges show their stuff, and once, he joined two other trumpeters around one mic for a hair-raising blow-out. Afterward, he sat for an hour or so and signed autographs for bedazzled high school students, band kids who'd just been treated to some historic showmanship.

Another jazz show that was more bluegrass and rock featured Béla Fleck, the leader and namesake of the inimitable Flecktones, who normally play velvet-seat venues.

We booked Béla thanks to an intern working for us at the time. Charlie Jennings, then a senior at Wofford College in Spartanburg, was a die-hard music fan whose easygoing demeanor and clean-cut good looks belied his taste for metal and hardcore. He was a huge fan of Metallica, with whom he would later snag an even better internship.

Before he joined us that semester, I asked him: "So, what makes you think you should work here?"

"I can get you Béla Fleck."

Un-hunh, and I can have coffee with Charlize Theron. " 'Zat so?"

"Yeah, I promoted a Béla show in Knoxville once, and I still have his agent's contact information."

And so he did: Joe Brauner worked in the Manhattan office of the powerhouse Creative Artists Agency, where he represented the likes of Norah Jones and Amos Lee. As far as my talent-buying experience went, Joe was out of our league. Apparently, he wasn't out of Charlie's.

A month later, a contract for a Béla Fleck performance sat on our desk.

Béla's show also featured banjo hero Tony Trischka, and they jammed and hammed it up for nearly three hours. At one point, the two played one banjo at the same time. Mind-boggling.

Despite the potentially humbling fact that Charlie was "just" a college kid, he taught me a lot that spring. He offered tips about dealing with major agents, and he designed our Offer Sheet, the formal document a promoter sends to agents in order to buy their artists. Charlie's Excel spreadsheet helped me dial in our show costs, which include everything from the artist's guarantee to our production expenses. That alone saved us incalculable sums of money that we should have been earning all along, if I had been using his industry-standard formulas in all my deals. After he graduated, he landed a job with the Southeast's biggest independent promoter, AC Entertainment, where he soon landed a role in booking Bonnaroo, the festival that has drawn upwards of ninety-thousand fans every year.

In addition to finding rapture in some of the music and unraveling some of the industry's complexities, I occasionally found myself amused and sometimes just plain baffled with the unusual species known as artists.

John Mayall, for instance. Sure, he had introduced some of the biggest names in blues and rock during the last four decades. He was also known, among other things, for having owned one of the world's biggest collections of historic pornography, including some items that dated to the thirteenth century, until a house fire destroyed most of it.

One night, before one of his rollicking shows, I brought his supper to the dressing room—something along the lines of meatloaf and green beans and mashed potatoes. I watched him pull a large Ziploc bag from his knapsack and proceed to dump the entire contents of his plate into the baggie. He then sealed it and stuffed it into his luggage.

The next morning, he needed a ride to the airport. His band was traveling separately and would meet him later. It was too cold and too early, but I had offered to take him; nobody else was available at that hour. Before picking him up at the Hyatt, I stopped at Krispy Kreme for a half a dozen glazed doughnuts and two large coffees. During the five-minute drive downtown, I sipped my coffee and munched on one of the hot, fresh treats. A few minutes later, in the lobby, I gave him the other coffee and showed him the box, whereupon he pulled another Ziploc baggie from his knapsack, dumped the remaining five doughnuts inside and stuffed them into his carry-on.

Another time, just a year after we opened, the great Keb' Mo' returned. Apparently, he had just been in Colorado, where two of our delightful original servers, Effie and Stacey, had gone skiing. They came back and told us that they were hitchhiking from the slope one afternoon, back to wherever it was they were staying. A car pulled over, and they climbed in.

"Hey," Stacey said, "aren't you Keb' Mo'?"

He smiled and said that, yes, he was.

"You just played our place! The Handlebar!"

In fact, he had, and he would one last time before he got a role in TV's *Touched By An Angel*, won a couple of Grammies and appeared in a few films.

The second time he appeared, he was beyond generous.

"It's really nice to be back here at The Handlebar," he told the sold-out crowd. "This is one of those special rooms, y'know, it's a real cool place."

And at the end of his show, he did what no performer had ever done before—he welcomed his opening act to join him on stage. We had added a young musician named Evan Dehner to the bill. At the time, Evan was maybe sixteen years old, a stringy, pimply teenager, but he could play a National-steel guitar with the poise and chops of a road-weary veteran. He blew harp like an accomplished blues hound, and he sang with the voice of an eighty-year-old black man. (Not long afterward, we heard that Evan had run off to a commune in

Oregon or somewhere in the Great Northwest. I would have to guess that his preternatural talent was even too intense for him.)

On another memorable occasion, Leftover Salmon spent the day clowning around the mill. The afternoon was gorgeous, so the guys clambered up the water tower and found their way into the cupola. Somewhere along the road, they had commandeered a Mayor McCheese from some McDonald's; the fiberglass figure was about as big around as a tractor tire. They hauled it to the top of the mill and heaved it from the cupola because, they said, "We wanted to see if he could fly." Later, during their show, they Duct-taped themselves together because, they said, they believed in "taping a good show."

Meanwhile, life inside the mill and out was turning out to be about as smooth as a Coltrane epic from his avant-garde phase.

A few standouts dotted our 1998 calendar, namely Arlo Guthrie; the Amazing Rhythm Aces, with their '70s classic, "Third Rate Romance"; and Guster, a quirky Boston band that would eventually explode. And in 1999, our last full year at Mills Centre, Robin Trower blew up the joint with "Bridge of Sighs" and a few hits from his Procol Harum days; Leon Russell returned; and Jesse Winchester joined Guy Clark in the year's most cherished show.

Otherwise, hostilities with the landlord escalated, along with the country's "irrational exuberance"—a tension bubble that would have to blow up somewhere… and on someone.

During that same spring, I began to feel new, increased pain in my left hip, where I had undergone replacement surgery exactly ten years before. Since I was so good at denying discomfort, Kathy finally dragged me to see a doctor. Sure enough, the very problem that surgeons had predicted would happen happened: The prosthetic hip had failed. I needed a new one to replace the replacement.

Kathy and I decided to return to the original surgeon, in Orlando, Florida, which kept us farther away from the business than either of us wanted to be and for much longer than we wanted to be there.

The operation itself went well, and we returned home, but not long afterward, at the start of my six-week recuperation period, I developed a blood clot. Clotting is a relatively common complication after a procedure that requires you to stay off your feet, even though the doctor and physical therapists had prescribed exercises to help prevent them. I just didn't do any. The throbbing in my left calf felt like nothing more than a bad charley horse, but, once again, Kathy insisted on taking me to Greenville Memorial Hospital's Emergency Room. One of our longtime friends and patrons, Dr. Ed, happened to be on duty that day. He immediately diagnosed the clot and, with grave relief, explained how it could have floated up into my heart. He saved my life.

The entire episode was hard enough, but when August rolled around, we experienced our first-ever spate of show cancellations.

We had always known that any time an artist or agent calls off a show, we had no recourse. Contracts see to that. The legally binding documents originate from the agencies, not the talent buyer, so they bend over backwards to protect their clients and themselves, not the promoter. Let's say that the artist gets a last-minute invitation to appear on *Letterman*, or the band's tour bus breaks down. Oh, well. But if any promoter makes the mistake of canceling a show, for *any* reason, he generally gets hit for the fifty-percent non-refundable deposit, along with multiple threats from agents who scream that "we'll never do business with your scuzzy ass again."

So we were powerless through a month-long series of canceled shows. The first one came from the up-and-coming blues singer, Shemekia Copeland, the daughter of the mighty blues guitarist Johnny Copeland. Shemekia called to say that her band's van had broken down seven hours away. She called four hours before their advertised show time. A couple of weeks later, Cowboy Mouth, the hurricane-force New Orleans rockers, scuttled their show. Through the rest of that August, we suffered a few other no-shows. We could do nothing but try and book a last-minute, fill-in band, while quietly complaining to nobody and counting the losses from the money that we had spent to promote shows that never happened.

Sort of like a death-row inmate who can only wait for the end, we knew it was coming and we didn't know when. Time was running out for us at the mill.

As it turned out, our business had one year left.

Kathy and I had no idea what we would do once we were finally thrown out of the space. So we just kept trying to do what we'd been doing for the past six years, promoting shows and coming up with creative ways to put butts in seats.

Since the beginning, we had tried all manner of things, from children's shows to poetry slams to contra dances, but our best and most favorite events proved to be benefit concerts. We liked putting them on—that is, we let any number of brand-name organizations take over our venue. We figured that any charity needing to raise money would have to work as hard as we always did to promote their shows. These nonprofits then not only filled a night here and there in our calendar, they also freed us from having to take booking risks. Plus, these shows mostly packed our room; we earned our take from bar sales. We also chalked up gold stars in the community for our largesse.

Our first benefit, as a matter of fact, materialized just three weeks after we opened. Right out of the gate, Gene Berger offered to hold a fundraising concert for WNCW, the public radio station in nearby Spindale, North Carolina. WNCW had opened five years before we did and played the same music that Gene sold at his store and we promoted in our room. To headline the benefit, Gene landed on Dave Alvin, the California rocker who co-founded The Blasters with his brother, Phil. Dave had already established himself as a leading pioneer of "Americana," which often means "country-tinged rock that you can understand the words to."

The show was a success for everyone, paving the way for our appreciation of benefit shows.

Through the years, we offered fundraisers for the Sierra Club, Red Cross, the Children's Hospital and a community-service organization called Compass of Carolina, a United Way agency that began sponsoring "Chase Away the Blues." Yes, two nights of blues—but blues shows that almost always sold out.

Our wildest fundraisers, which also helped WNCW, will likely remain our most memorable: "Dylan for Dollars," "Beatles for Bucks" and "Cash for Cash." Each show, of course, paid tribute to the title artist, and for each, we enlisted more than a dozen bands and solo artists—rock bands, bluegrass bands, jazz bands, punk bands, singer/songwriters and even a chamber ensemble. The participants got to choose, first-come, first-served, one or two songs from the vast catalogue of the evening's featured artist. Then they covered those tunes with their own interpretation; the chamber quartet delivered a haunting rendition of "Eleanor Rigby."

All the bands used the same backline—a drum kit and bass and guitar amps—to minimize the technical logistics for our sound guy and stage manager, who ushered the performers on and off the stage after their allotted five- to seven-minute mini-sets. Somehow, these well-oiled productions of choreographic ingenuity ran on time, often even ahead of schedule.

At our first attempt at one of these clusters, "Dylan for Dollars," the quirky Asheville, North Carolina, performer, Billy Jonas, fronted a nine-piece band that played "Subterranean Homesick Blues" on everything from guitars to garbage cans, and one guy blew an entire verse through a garden hose. Capping off the show, The Blow Up, one of Greenville's punk stalwarts, unleashed a blistering version of "Like A Rolling Stone."

When the inevitable Notice of Eviction finally hit us, then, Kathy and the staff decided on one last fundraiser. For ourselves. After all, with no business and nowhere else to go, we also would have no income.

We planned our last night at the mill with the ultimate tribute:

Johnny Cash. Proceeds from the Cash bash would finance the John and Kathy Homeless Venue and Personal Survival Fund.

Duwan Dunn, one of our longtime staff members and friends, planned the whole thing. She signed up all the bands and arranged who would play what song(s) and when.

Throughout the emotion-packed night, fans were treated to the craziest versions of "Folsom Prison Blues" and "Ballad of a Teenage Queen." Sometime during the proceedings, Duwan stopped everything and held a candlelight vigil, as much for Kathy and me as for the old mill and our beloved Handlebar.

Friends and patrons passed a candle and shared stories: "I have so many memories here …" "Thank you for doing all that you've done …" Tears flowed hard. Warmth and intimacy and concern and appreciation filled the room, along with the glowing flickers. All that work, all that sacrifice and everything we were about to lose somehow became, in those magical moments, meaningful and worthwhile, even redemptive.

And then The Blow Up delivered the walloping finale with their incendiary take on "Ring of Fire."

Thanks to everyone that night, Kathy and I took home about five-thousand dollars—all the money that we would have to live on until we could determine what to do next.

The following day, we returned with a platoon of helpful friends to finish clearing out of the mill. We felt washed out, and our last moments in those rooms felt brutal as a burial. We watched trucks and cars packed with boxes, furniture, files and equipment—all to be stored in a warehouse that our friend, Bill, had donated to us—as if we were witnessing a funeral cortège bearing away our very souls.

As we dismantled The Handlebar and the rooms emptied, we could practically see and hear the countless memories.

Finally, when everything was gone and everyone had left, Kathy and I lingered alone. We stood together in sad and hopeless wonder.

I leaned into my wife and sobbed. "What now?"

"Stay with this," she said. She shed a tear or two, but remained impossibly stoic.

We left the mill and locked the doors.

When we drove away, we could only hope that everything we had left in the mill—the songs and sounds, the crowds and conversations—would cling to the beams and bricks along with the old lint from all that cotton that had built the place a hundred years before.

6

After we lost our space, we didn't lose our company.

The subsequent months took on an uncanny resemblance to those stressed-out days in 1994, when we first ramped up our business.

While we had time now to consider our next step, we also had plenty to do. Kathy and I turned our energies on the company that we *did* have and what we could to do to salvage it. (Stephen had since bowed out to focus on his family and career, attending to his marriage and raising his daughter.) With few, if any, other ideas or real or palatable options, my wife and I worked toward a future that would return us to full-time music promotion—along with even greater liabilities, long hours and that same ol' stress.

Days after we left the mill, a longtime friend, Chris, offered us a small office, rent free, in a building he owned. The room, about the size of a master-bedroom closet, soon held a desk, phone, fax machine and filing cabinet. We went to work, almost as if we had real jobs. We filled our days seeking partners, shopping for real estate, talking to potential investors and bankers. At one point, we even gathered two dozen friends and fans in a roundtable, taking in their advice.

For better or for worse, we kept hanging on. Perhaps our reasons—or maybe just *my* reasons—remained as ineluctable as destiny or fate or legacy. All the while, though, I felt as if I moved through the day in an insoluble daze, confused, disappointed, relieved, unhinged and ambivalent. Was this perilous music-business game really worth playing—again? I preferred not to think about what lay ahead, but I had to plan *something*. What about a job at some PR firm in town or, perish the thought, working at the local paper? What marketable skills did I really have? Let's see: saloon owner, music promoter and (sober) journalist.

My future seemed to come down to a question I either was too afraid to ask or just didn't want to solve: Was my *real* purpose in life really to provide people good music in a Southern city that was now booming? The Germans had moved in with BMW, joining Michelin and other global brands in investing millions and hiring thousands here. We even began seeing major national retailers and exotic eateries pop up—Thai, Vietnamese, Indian. Gone were the days when IHOP led the Best International Restaurant awards.

These were new times that offered new opportunity.

But were they? And was it?

Our primary goal was to find a bigger venue in a better location. We wanted to be where the action was—downtown. Greenville's tree-lined Main Street was sprucing up, blossoming in popularity and national attention. Long-shuttered buildings began opening up with fancy restaurants and independent retailers. At the same time, another district, the historic West End, at Main Street's southern terminus, began attracting serious attention from businesspeople and City leaders.

When we had first arrived in town, you just didn't go to the West End. Many of its century-old buildings sat vacant, with dilapidated façades and shattered windows. The area crawled with the poor, crack heads and alcoholics, the homeless and the hippies, along with yuppies slumming at Casablanca's, the popular dive bar that happened to be another one of Jud's cash-pumping properties.

The City was hatching big plans. The West End sat on the banks of the Reedy River, whose dramatic falls, rocky outcroppings and lush parks bestowed ripe development opportunities. The local government invested heavily in what it now christened, if perhaps prematurely, its "arts and entertainment district."

That was where we needed to be. We wanted to join the parade of entrepreneurs who were opening chi-chi galleries and boutiques, high-end fern bars and bistros.

But right before our eyes, the real estate rush pushed lease rates higher and higher, with landlords placing ever heavier bets on City Hall's rapid-fire renewal campaign. Every time we looked at a potential venue, the costs rose. Windows of opportunity closed as fast as they opened. Even the Mayor, who initiated and nurtured the West End's boom, sounded empathetic when I ran into him one day on Main Street. He gazed south toward his signature project and told me about The Gap, the national blue-jeans retailer:

"They were looking at a place down there, but even *they* complained about the square-footage rates quoted to them. Way out of line. So they decided to move to downtown Charleston."

Really? That's some serious speculative hubris, when rents even exceeded those in the heart of the South's Holy City.

Meanwhile, a new music venue, Occasionally Blues, opened in the West End Market, a former cotton warehouse smack in the district's crossroads. The City had spent seven-and-a-half million dollars to renovate the building, in hopes of attracting private investors. So City Hall played the landlord when it leased part of the space to the new blues club and Southern-cuisine restaurant. (As far as I was concerned, the name alone would determine its fate: Occasionally Blues operated under the premise that offering live blues and fine dining would actually sustain a concert venue. But I wasn't about to tell anyone else that.)

Still, Kathy and I admired the new owners, a generous and brilliant businessman named Jerry, his charming wife, Brenda, and their son-in-law, Rob. We liked them so much that we gave more than a passing thought to joining them. We figured that since The Handlebar's multi-genre menu had worked all this time, why, we could fuse our music-promotion model with Jerry's business acumen to create a stronger enterprise. Many an evening, Kathy and I joined Jerry and Rob on the restaurant's back porch, enjoying the fine Upstate weather and some delicious—and complimentary—food as we tried to work out a mutually beneficial plan. Through all of these discussions, we landed on a stopgap idea: Kathy and I would promote a few shows there. We promised to pack the place, which would give their cash registers a boost and keep The Handlebar's name in the public eye, while giving us a shot at earning a little money.

Our first concert there headlined none other than Leon Redbone, our original marquee star who had unwittingly driven me to my first major meltdown. This time around, we didn't provide all that ridiculous hospitality, but while Leon had no trouble voicing his displeasure at the restaurant's lack of dressing rooms, he still put on a great show. The place was packed. We made a few bucks.

Next up was Fred Eaglesmith, one of my longtime personal favorites, a Zen cowboy from southern Ontario. He brought his trademark story-songs and off-kilter Canadian banter to a crowd comprised mostly of orphaned Handlebar fans; our now-unemployed ex-staffer, Duwan, had recently told Kathy: "Y'know, without The Handlebar, these people are wandering around town with nowhere else to go and nothing to do."

Then came Seven Nations, which had sold out our old room several times. As usual, their fans flocked in, from as far away as Maryland and Texas, from virtually every surrounding state. And they blew up Occasionally Blues with their Scots/Irish rock and wailing bagpipes and a front man blessed with sterling vocals and movie-star good looks. We had warned Jerry and Rob that Seven Nations would shatter their business's admissions and bar records. Sure enough, not long after the band loaded in its own complete PA system, the place hit wall-to-wall capacity. And afterward, the exhausted, exhilarated staff said they had never experienced anything like it. Everyone earned some money that night.

With our confidence boosted, Kathy and I thought to branch out, think big, go bigger.

New Year's Eve was coming. But not just any New Year's Eve. This was going to be 2000, the turn of the century, the end of a transformative and challenging and exhilarating decade.

We turned to longtime friends, Cravin' Melon, one of the area's most successful bands. In those days, Cravin', as their "Melon-head" fans called them, had been riding the coattails of Hootie & The Blowfish, the newly minted superstars from Columbia. We knew that we could parlay Cravin's radio-friendly popularity into a big event, regardless of the even bigger risks.

In earnest, we began working with the band's manager/producer, Dick Hodgin, and we approached another upstart band, Albert Hill, a well-known group from Spartanburg that would surely add value to the bill. At one of their own headlining shows at the mill, Albert Hill had sold more tickets than any other band, busting our official capacity by more than three-hundred fans; even the vast parking lot overflowed that night. Like Cravin' Melon, Albert Hill also employed a risk-ready manager, a smart, even visionary Greenville transplant named Marty Winsch. (Marty, who fast become one of my closest friends, later went on to manage Corey Smith and become a player in the industry.)

For the venue, we chose Greenville's sprawling Expo Center, a cavernous exhibition hall normally used for gun-and-knife shows, boat shows and bridal shows, and, a few years later, a temporary shelter for Hurricane Katrina refugees.

The event's total upfront costs were daunting: a stout rental fee, festival-sized staging, a big PA and lighting rig and the crew to set it all up and operate it; ample security and a couple of paramedics. We even purchased snow insurance from a company that underwrote such things. At the same time, the Expo Center's deal cut us out of any income from the all-important concessions, so ticket sales would be crucial if we had any hope of recouping those thick costs and hoping to make a thin dime.

By the time the clock struck midnight, more than seven hundred and fifty people were on hand to support the bands and the still-displaced Handlebar—more than double the crowd that we could have accommodated in the mill or at Occasionally Blues. Kathy and I earned a few dollars then, too.

Not long afterward, Occasionally Blues changed ownership.

So much for *that* option.

Now we were reaching the bottom of our fiscal and emotional barrel. Time was running out for us to find any opportunity, never mind an *ideal* one.

Then one afternoon, Kathy mentioned the name of a former computer-company owner who had thrown a couple of lucrative office parties at The Handlebar. We learned that he had recently sold his business, so we figured that he might be looking for another prospect or perhaps just something else to do. That day, Kathy said with exasperated finality: "Okay, one more phone call, one last shot at this. If he says no, he says no, and we change course altogether."

Seemed like the most sensible plan. I picked up the phone.

Our friends, Herb and Carol Ireland, had been longtime regulars at the mill. They dropped in every now and then, chain-smoked—they ultimately quit—and enjoyed a few glasses of white Zin. Herb was an engineer who designed production-line robots. He was really smart; still is. He knew business; still does. He knew people, too. He had always been far too generous with us. One weekend, he enlisted a friend to expand our minuscule stage. He drew up the plans, spent two full, long, exhausting days banging nails and hauling boards, and he charged us nothing but our undying appreciation.

Not long after my last-ditch call to our would-be partner, I phoned Herb to ask his advice.

The Irelands took us to lunch at a linen-tablecloth restaurant, where Herb took out his mechanical pencil and began doodling on a beverage napkin.

"The only thing I can tell you," he said, "is that several years ago, we got into business with some partners, some investors. The trouble was that, okay, yes, they'd been friends of ours, but we didn't know anything about them, really. I mean, they were actually just acquaintances, but the point is, we didn't *know anything about them*. Needless to say, it didn't take long for us to realize just how little we knew about them, until things started to go…well, not very well." He peered over his glasses, at once paternal and professorial, caring and concerned. "What I'm saying is: Do *not* get into bed with anyone unless you know absolutely everything about them. *Everything*. Ab. So. Lutely. Every. Thing."

But we had run out of options, along with time and money and everything else.

Next thing you know, Kathy and I belonged to a revived company with new partners.

After meetings, handshakes and agreements, she and I realized, immediately, that we knew…absolutely nothing about these men. Not only had we failed to exploit our considerable, if now-rusty, reportorial skills to learn as much about them as we could, but worse than that, we ignored Herb's warning. Soon enough, we were in bed with Yankee "bidnessmen," though it wasn't two months before we realized that we had traded our dream to precisely the wrong people. In any case, the less said about them, the better and, perhaps even, safer.

Our new little syndicate said that they would go into business with us only if we—they—purchased a building. They refused to sign any lease on somebody else's property, only to pump hundreds of thousands of dollars into upgrading it. In for a penny, they said, in for a pound.

Now with something akin to financing in our back pocket, we soon found a place that looked promising.

The building sat at the edge of downtown, at the exact opposite end of Main Street from the hoppin' West End. While the so-called North Main area wasn't one of Greenville's hot spots, the location was still plenty conspicuous, even though its four-lane thoroughfare, Stone Avenue, had fallen on hard times.

On either side of Stone, neighborhoods of quiet tree-laden streets were dotted with occasional mansions and lined with tidy bungalows. During the 1940s and '50s, North Main was considered "the suburbs"; downtown was within walking distance. At the same time, the sputtering Stone Avenue corridor included a few filling stations and a restaurant or two, a pharmacy, a Pet Dairy and bus depot. At one end of the street, a Sears & Roebuck now stood empty.

The building right next door to the old Sears campus just then hit the market.

The hulking gray structure looked a bit like a World War II-era naval cargo ship run aground. The building had opened fifty years before as an Oldsmobile dealership. Much later, an auto-body shop moved in. The shop parked wrecked cars behind the building in a small, unsightly backyard that also served as an impound lot for cars that had been towed from late-night drivers who had been tossed in the County's drunk tank, only a few blocks away.

The building's interior looked ideal. The floor plan would allow us to build a separation between our bar/restaurant, just inside the front entrance, and our concert space in the rear. Our partners insisted on installing a full-service kitchen, complete with a grill, fryers, a hood system, the whole works—in other words, a new undertaking far exceeding anyone's expertise.

In the front half, a former owner had built a mezzanine apartment, complete with a bedroom, full bath and a small living room, none of which could have been legal under the area's zoning rules. Still, our architect decided to retain segments of the upper level, including the shower—touring artists love that perk—and space for a Skybox, with tables and chairs that overlooked the garage. The garage, whose concrete floor once held new Chevys and still included diagonal yellow parking stripes, would serve as our Listening Room. There, an arched ceiling rose some twenty feet, which would provide bands plenty of head room, while its steel trellises would be great for hanging stage lights and big speakers.

The room looked big enough. The larger capacity could conceivably at least double our revenues—a notion that proved to be a bit less naïve than our original predictions six years before.

We were onto something now. The partners seemed amenable enough, the building looked suitable enough, and the location appeared workable enough.

Then we ran into the neighbors.

Never mind that when we took possession of the building, homeless people wandered up and down Stone Avenue, from a soup kitchen on one end to low-rent housing on the other. Along the way, one business paid for plasma, another found work for day laborers. The corridor itself was lined with cracked sidewalks, littered with broken bottles and cigarette butts, and yet the street bisected Greenville's hippest uptown residential areas.

At first glance, City officials believed that a private, million-dollar investment in the old auto-body shop—and a business that would bring thousands of people to North Main's wobbly commercial strip—seemed like a good idea. Greenville police even cited the so-called Shattered Glass Theory, applied to an area that's mired in dilapidated buildings, busted windows and broken lives, a place wallowing in violence and hopelessness. Conversely, they said, a cleaned-up building or city block, so the theory went, fixed all that.

Police trumpeted the rebirth of the south Bronx and, closer to home, the West End. But Stone Avenue was no south Bronx.

As soon as we moved in, a posse of neighbors began to get anxious, giving City officials second thoughts in the face of a classic government dilemma: commercial development vs. residential expectations.

Our new ownership group had already signed mountains of loan documents, but none of us realized just how much our move would inspire a neighborhood uprising.

At the old mill, we had worked in near-total autonomy, thanks to our shattered-glass environs. Now, though, we had landed smack in the middle of two neighborhoods that—wouldn't you know?—were designated Registered Historic Districts. A police lieutenant once told me, way back in my days reporting for the *St. Petersburg Times*: "When you're dealing with poor neighborhoods, housing projects, the disenfranchised and whatnot, you get calls from residents about drug-dealing, shootings, overdoses, stolen cars and assorted violence. But when you're dealing with moneyed white folks, you get complaints about the color of the Dumpsters."

We collided head-on with NIMBY—Not In My Back Yard.

Our new public-relations problem necessitated a charm offensive. We invited all the neighbors into our building, which had just begun to fill with blueprints and contractors, hammers and two-by-fours, drywall and power tools. We wanted to show everyone what fine, high-integrity businesspeople we were.

One chilly winter afternoon, we opened our doors, which hadn't quite been installed yet, to a half-dozen residents. We stood together in the middle of the saw-dusted garage. They listened to our presentation, which included handbills that detailed all the ways anyone could reach us anytime, day or night, to voice any concerns or problems. We promised to be good, nay, *great!*, neighbors who would revitalize the entire area. We would work to the best of our ability to handle such issues as noise, traffic and crowds. We would provide security and safe parking. We would control loitering and litter, even weeds.

They crossed their arms. They looked anxious and grim. The moment we stopped talking, a woman from across the street spoke up. She apparently had been designated the neighborhood jury's forewoman. She delivered their swift, unanimous verdict. Her eyes narrowed, her voice iced with rage, and she said:

"We appreciate the invitation and your promises of good intentions and even your reputation, but we will not stop fighting you until we shut you down."

One of their first opportunities to curb our evil designs came earlier than any of us had expected. Residents persuaded the City to enact parking restrictions on their streets so that anyone who parked without a permit in the newly designated zone would get a five-hundred—that's right, *five-hundred*—dollar fine.

The neighbors' next shot came when the City told us that we had to get approval to use a sliver of our own property for additional parking. We had naturally assumed that we could do pretty much what we wanted to with real estate, namely the back lot that, until recently, had been filled with wrecked and impounded cars. Silly us. To allow any cars behind our building, we would have to get a zoning variance. That meant a public hearing, which also meant that stoked-up neighbors could gang up and bitch on record.

Back in my days as a cub reporter, I used to cover these tedious and uneventful dog-and-pony shows. Now we sat in the center of one. The conference room in City Hall was packed, bitter residents on one side, supportive fans on the other.

The moment the board rejected our petition, the media went nuts. A news crew raced out to get reaction from the streets. As soon as the TV satellite van appeared in the cozy cul-de-sac, you would have thought that Santa Claus had just pulled up in an ice-cream truck. Children appeared from out of nowhere; we had never seen any of them before. But now here they were scooting around on their bikes and skateboards and playing ball with their dads, who were all typically still at work that time of day. The twilight seemed to have spontaneously erupted into one swell block party, even though it was suppertime.

The cameraman captured bucolic images amid the stately Tudor and Colonial homes, and Norman Rockwell sounds filled the tape. Over laughter of playful youths, the reporter intoned:

"To some people on this corner, *this* noise is part of what makes it (the neighborhood) so special."

He went on to interview a lawyer, who, gloating over their fresh City Hall victory, said, "I believe, seventeen children in the neighborhood (are) under the age of fourteen."

To which the reporter added: "Not far from this makeshift playground is an empty parking lot, and next door to that, a new concert hall… and not everyone is welcoming the new club."

Thus began a fight that would last for years and sap way too much energy and time from what we thought was supposed to be our mission: bring great music to a growing city.

With construction now fully underway, we threw ourselves back into the business of music. In late winter and early spring 2001, I began to book shows again. It felt good. At the same time, any bookings, especially the first one, hinged, once again, on the date that our contractor believed he could wrap up construction and obtain that crucial Certificate of Occupancy permit for us. How easy would it be for us to recreate the same train wreck that we had witnessed before Livingston Taylor's show seven years before?

The agreed-upon timeline called for our Grand Reopening in mid-May.

This time around, we opted for a "soft" opener, choosing a proven box-office winner over some huge, cutting-edge rock band that would rattle our rafters and shred our already-frayed nerves. So we returned to our roots when we decided to go after the ever-reliable rocker

Dave Alvin. I had always liked and enjoyed working with Dave and his band, The Guilty Men, and Dave's agent, Brad Madison, who ran Mongrel Music, a boutique agency, so-called for its comparatively small and selective roster of artists. I could always count on Brad to reach a reasonable deal with us. For years, I had bought numerous dates from him, low-risk shows with his other artists, including Saffire: The Uppity Blues Women, Chris Smither, Steve Forbert, Los Straitjackets and a few more. With Brad, I knew that we would have a successful concert, and with Dave, I knew that our first night would be stress-free.

Dave and his band put on one hell of a show. And Dave himself was one of those talented pros who didn't pose as a rock star, a down-to-earth road veteran who slipped on a pair of work gloves and joined the rest of his band in loading in their own gear. Their needs were always simple, even a pleasure to provide. And to top all that off, Dave had just won his first Grammy Award only the year before for Best Traditional Folk Album, our métier.

Dave once told a reporter, "There are two kinds of folk music, quiet folk music and loud folk music. I play both"—a comment that called to mind one of his shows back at the old mill.

In one of Dave's earliest shows for us, he and his Guilty Men had started their set off a little slow, kind of low-key, with a ballad or two. Once he got the feel of the room and the sound, he gained more and more control over the crowd. Then the band picked up the pace and volume. Soon, the songs moved like roller coaster cars, climbing an emotional incline one minute and hurling into a rockin' free fall the next.

While I watched Dave Alvin & The Guilty Men ricochet through roots-rock, Tejano/conjunto and boot-scootin' country, I was also keeping my eye on a guy who looked like he was about to go apeshit. During one high-velocity song, the man grabbed a pair of chairs, not fancy chairs, by any means, just the stackable kind with cheap padding over pressboard seats. He began tapping them on the mill's indestructible wood floors. When Dave and the band lifted from ballad to blast-off, the man went from tapping the chairs to pounding them along with the ratcheting beat. He kept pounding and pounding the chairs, until finally, on the last note, he let them go. They dropped like squished spiders, dead, their black legs sprawled out, crushed. Dumbfounded, I looked at the spent fan, who was beaming with the same ecstasy that makes you forget just about everything.

"You're an animal," I said.

He grinned back at me, still drunk on his own hundred-proof adrenaline. "Yea-uh. Huh-huh. Hell of a show." He clapped me on the shoulder and walked away without picking up the chairs, shaking his head and muttering, "Yup, a-yep, one *hell* of a show."

So except for the occasional crazed fan, all we had to look forward to on the afternoon of May 16, 2001, was a comparatively easy slide into our new home, with Dave's show set to start at eight-thirty p.m.

Life, of course, had another schedule.

The day began taking on that ominous feeling of déjà vu.

Three months after construction had started, the clock now ticked inexorably toward our five p.m. opening. City Building inspectors arrived for a final look. Along with the Fire Marshal—the hawk-eyed Mr. Cook had retired by now—they scrutinized every piece of wiring, every fire extinguisher and exit sign, every door and latch, the staging, the sound-baffling curtains. They went through all the same motions we had seen them go through at the mill. The contractors and subs followed them around like rock groupies. Everyone knew, just as we had learned years before, that without City approval, we would have no Occupancy permit. No Occupancy permit, no show.

As the punch lists grew and tensions rose, the band loaded in. Kathy and our new staff scurried about, putting the finishing touches on the bar and, now, restaurant. I did what I always did best. I wandered around, aimless, helpless, useless and stressed.

Then five p.m. came. And went.

Fans, friends, well-wishers—everyone began showing up outside our door. But the City's Building Inspector, Steve Landrith, a big man with a builder's paunch and brisket-thick hands, wasn't quite ready to issue that golden permit, not until...

"Okay, here's the deal," he finally said. "We've got a few issues, mostly wiring, here and there, and some other things that need to be worked out, but this is what we can do."

None of that sounded all that promising. Time was up, my spirits weren't. We *had* to open. We *had* to put on a show. We *had* to start selling all that go-juice that would ultimately float us out of our colossal new debt—cold beer in longneck bottles and 1.7-ounce shots of booze from the little airplane-sized ones.

Mr. Landrith looked around and said that he could write a Temporary Occupancy Permit.

"A temporary Occu—uh, what's that?" I asked, my nerves fried.

"That means that we'll give y'all a certain amount of time to correct the problems on the list here, but . . ." He let the bad news sink in while he waved over his much-inked clipboard. "It also means that, well . . . We can authorize people in the building, that is, to legally *occupy* the space, but a Temporary Occupancy Permit's not sufficient to get your alcohol-beverage license."

"It's not . . . *what?*" We were about to have a rock concert without beer? Selling music is one thing. Selling booze, bottom line, is what the club business is all about: Selling bands without selling beer is bankruptcy.

"State law says—"

"But the state has already *approved* our beer and wine and liquor licenses," I said. "We went through all that already, we paid for them!"

"Right, yes, but the State won't issue a formal, *legal* license unless you have an official, *permanent* Occupancy Permit in hand."

Oh, for pity's sake!

Nobody had warned us about that particular possibility. We had spent the last several months going round and round with the

City on issues that ranged from zoning to parking to the appropriate shrubbery on our property. We had met with irate residents. We had appeared at contentious City hearings. We even planted—and replanted several times—a variety of costly shrubs to appease City officials and screen our property from residents.

Now, with customers returning for the first time since our enforced hiatus, we could let them in, sure, but with the news that they would leave thirsty.

As soon as Mr. Landrith handed over our *temporary* Certificate, I skulked through the concert hall and out the side door. I slid behind the Dumpster in our load-in zone. In the heat of that May afternoon, I released the same tension that had overwhelmed me the day when Livingston Taylor took our first stage.

Yes, I cried again. But I wondered: Were these tears this time of relief or rather of some prescient fear that we had gotten ourselves into something far deeper than we could have imagined?

The slightest inkling of an answer came several hours later, after Dave's show. In what had to be one of the most laid-back concerts in small-club history, thanks to the absence of alcohol, we sold only about half our capacity. Fans had each paid only twelve dollars apiece to attend our Grand Reopening. We earned not a dime.

And yet, almost in spite of ourselves, here we were, on our way. Again.

7

The glamour of the music business was giving way to more and bigger headaches, some of which we should have predicted would last for years. Plenty of them, of course, came with the territory, running a small business and from the music business itself, but a few provided abiding nuisances that had little to do with either.

One mighty, ongoing pain in the ass involved the neighbors. Not all of them, by any means, but, like, three or four of them. Maybe five, tops.

Our staunchest, most indefatigable nemesis lived with his family in a lovely two-story home nearby. The tree-shaded manse had originally belonged to one of Greenville's pioneering businessmen but now housed a husband and father who had once been a regular at the old mill. He was, or had been, anyway, a music fan; friends said he owned a massive stereo system, and his album collection apparently included many of the bands we promoted. He also worked from his house, an IT guy who knew his way around cyberspace and evidently had no other life.

We'll call him "Javert," after Victor Hugo's character, whose singular obsession with The Law became a bit, let's say, time-consuming. From the outset, the neighborhood's self-appointed "inspector" made it clear that his primary objective was to criminalize our existence. He figured he could do that by singlehandedly getting City Council to rewrite Greenville's *entire* Noise Ordinance.

For the next several months, which eventually stretched into years, he gathered mountains of data. He compiled everything from sound regulations in other communities to the decibel levels of water fountains, motorcycles and rock 'n' roll. He could recite a noise ordinance from some Oregon backwater and tell you the megahertz of bass waves. When he wasn't sitting at his computer and combing the Internet, he paced his estate night after night with his newest purchase: his own decibel meter.

We had already tried to defuse him. Early on, I knocked on his door, hoping to engage him in a friendly conversation and even extend a peace offering—free tickets and front-row seats for life. He barely opened his door.

Thereafter, he preferred to monitor the "noise" that he said emanated from our building. Any time his meter's needle hit a certain number, he dialed 911. His calls became constant. From the day we opened and through December 2002, three or four neighbors, but mostly Javert, called police *thirty-five* times, an average of about one call every other week. Most times, an officer stopped first at the complainant's home, where he checked things out, and then drove around to The Handlebar. With his eyes rolling, he told us to turn it down. We agreeably hustled to the sound booth, where we didn't do anything at all but simply waited for the show to end, which would be at about eleven or eleven-thirty p.m.

Still, the crying wolf got louder. Tensions escalated.

At one point, Javert finagled City officials into arranging a decibel-meter-reading party in his yard. The meeting was set for an evening in early November, just six months after we opened. Fourteen people showed up, including the City Manager; three police officers; an Assistant City Attorney; our sound engineer and our lawyer; the usual cabal of neighbors; and me. Police carried their own sound meter. Javert had his sound meter. Our sound guy, Andy, had one, too.

We also supplied a band. Inside our concert hall, Deep Banana Blackout was playing their sound check, with no idea what was going on outside. Meantime, the various participants stood around on Javert's lawn, where their decibel gauges showed readings that reached only as high as fifty-seven decibels—three points lower than the City's legal limit. I was asked to go back inside and make the band play louder.

"No," the lead singer told me, "this is about as loud as we get."

I pointed through the wall behind the band. "Well, see, we've got a bit of a problem in the neighborhood. I mean, I hate to ask you this, but y'all really are going to have to flat-out rock. The trouble seems to be that the cicadas are louder than you guys."

Flummoxed, the band simply walked off stage.

Next, I was told to tell our sound guy, Andy, to crank up a CD. *Really loud.* He picked Led Zeppelin. While he pushed the recorded music to ear-splitting levels in the empty concert hall, I returned to Javert's yard. Everyone continued fiddling with the meters. Still, Mother Nature kept interfering with the results.

The City's report later concluded:

"Sound readings taken inside The Handlebar ranged from 90 decibels on stage to a high of 103 decibels in the center of the room. The sound readings outside ranged from 51 to 56 decibels while the CD was playing . . . The residents concluded that sound was not a problem under the circumstances set forth this evening."

Not the least bit set back, Javert continued to seek justice.

A few months later, a City bureaucrat called The Handlebar to invite me to participate in a new "Noise Ordinance Advisory Committee."

Sure, I said, I had nothing better to do—other than, say, dig our company out of colossal debt and work at my job booking bands.

"But here's the thing," I also told the City guy, "I am not about to sit on some dopey, needless City committee if Javert's going to be on it, too."

"Of course, that's understandable."

"No, I'm serious. If you want to make this whole thing about The Handlebar and Javert, that's all well and good [it wasn't], but, in my opinion, a simple two-party misunderstanding shouldn't be the concern of a formal City committee. Still, if y'all *really* want to look at improving the *whole* noise ordinance *everywhere* in the City, I s'pose I could help with that." I stopped for a second, then added: "But, y'know, really, I'm just not sure that's necessary."

He said he would mail me a list of selected participants, culled from neighborhood associations and the business community, maybe a dozen people in all.

I soon received the invitation and recognized the names of several proposed panelists. None of them, as far as I knew, had any dog in this fight. The good news was that, as promised, Javert wasn't listed.

But when the bureaucrat-in-charge called the committee's first meeting, I read the names of all those invited. Wouldn't you know? Javert's name was there, too.

A bit pissed off, I phoned City Hall immediately. "You lied to me."

"No," he said, "just a miscommunication, is all."

For the next several months, Javert and I sat with a small group in a City Hall conference room to discuss the "noise situation" in the ever-expanding metropolis and weigh the possibilities of an outright rewrite of the all-encompassing ordinance.

At the first meeting, a police lieutenant briefed us about the scope of the "problem." He distributed a report showing that the department had responded to an average of a hundred and fifteen noise complaints citywide every month during a specific nine-month period. Of all those calls and complaints, he said, only *forty-seven*, or about half of one-percent, stemmed from bars and nightclubs.

"One of the biggest problems," he said, "is roosters. We get a lot of complaints about roosters."

The Noise Ordinance Advisory Committee meetings continued. So did Javert's calls to 911.

One balmy night in the middle of March 2004, fully *three years* after we moved in, another Responding Officer wrote in his police report:

> "I stood near the porch on the driveway at this residence. The (decibel) reading was conducted and the results again fluctuated between 55 and 60+, again depending on the rhythm and beat of the music…Shortly thereafter, we were approached by the owner, John Jeter. I asked him if he knew why we were there. He stated, 'Someone throwing up in the parking lot?' I advised him that it was a noise complaint. He stated that he had just conducted his own readings and his noise meter reflected 56. Sgt. Riggs advised him that by his own admission he was in violation. He replied, 'Yeah, but by only one (decibel).' The subject was advised that he would be charged under stated Section Code 16–92. While discussing the charge, the subject advised me he was familiar, because he is on the Noise Ordinance Board. I asked Mr. Jeter how we can solve this problem in the future. He stated, 'I am not going to comment.'"

The report went on to say that "a female"—that would have been my ever-sensible, level-headed wife and business partner, Kathy—came out to deal with the situation. In other words, she arrived to save me from myself. She told police that we had done everything possible to abate sound. In fact, she told him, we would be willing to shut down the whole shootin' match, right then and there. I refused to do that, the report said, because the band had "one more song left."

"While discussing the fine amount, Mr. Jeter commented that there is not a set fine as of yet, and that this
section code is directed specifically to shutting him down.
Mr. Jeter was given a courtesy summons and advised of his
court date and time."

Yes, the report did say that I had mouthed off to a police officer in
particular and, yes, that I was a smart-ass in general. But what it *didn't*
say was that I had also turned into a full-on Drama Queen, right there
in the middle of the street. During my set-to with the cops, I held my
wrists together and stuck my arms out toward the *two* patrol cruisers
that were parked in front of Javert's house.

"Arrest me!" I pleaded with them. "Handcuff me, and take me
away! I'm serious! Just let me call the newspaper on my way to the
clink."

I had had enough. I wanted the world to know that I was going to
jail for violating the law … by…*one* decibel!

What're you in for, pal? Noise. How bad? Can't say—do you have
any idea what *one* decibel sounds like? No, you don't, because that's
as close to silence as any scientific measurement can get.

As for the summons and court date? Well, our ever-amazing,
interminably patient and workaday-brilliant attorney, Frank Eppes, a
highly respected criminal-defense lawyer and the son of a prominent
judge, bailed me out of that, too.

At last, near the end of our years-long ordeal, I was finally
required to attend mediation with Javert. While I was never told the
consequences if I refused to attend, I did tell the City bureaucrat—
the same official who had helmed the now-fizzled Noise Ordinance
Advisory Committee—that I would humor them all again, but on
one condition:

"Look, I'll go to this mediation thing, but once all these sessions
are over, to everyone's satisfaction, the whole *thing* is over. All of it.
No *mas*. No more. No more meetings, no more 911 calls and police
visits, no more nothin'. We good with that?"

For six Tuesdays, I sat across from Javert in a small conference

John Jeter, even today an avid cyclist.

The author (right) and his brother pose for a poignant photo immediately after Stephen gave his brother the kidney that saved John's life.

Bride and groom pose after their Florida nuptials before their life-altering move to Greenville, SC.

The original home of The Handlebar, known as Mills Mill, was organized by Capt. Otis Prentiss Mills and began operation in 1887 with 8,000 spindles. Photo courtesy of Dr. Marshall D. Williams

What powered the old mill proved to be attractive landmarks to funk-seeking dreamers.

Country crooner Mark Collie sings to a packed house in the mill's atmospherically intriguing "listening room."
Photo by John Hoffman

A camera's flash lights up the usually dim ramp leading to the venue in Mills Centre.

Jeter introduces one of nearly three thousand bands The Handlebar has promoted.

Author's brother, Stephen Jeter, and wife, Kathy Laughlin, share a few minutes at the original Handlebar when they're not working the crowds.
Photo by Debbie Knebel

Horizon Productions presents...

Keb' Mo'

with special guest
Evan Dehner

Friday, November 10, 1995
8:30 p.m.
Tickets: $12

the Handlebar

A
LISTENING
ROOM
Mills Centre
400 Mills Avenue
Greenville, SC
(803) 233-6173

Keb Mo's second show features young local prodigy Evan Dehner— for all of $12.

Spartanburg-area bluesmen Freddie Vanderford and Brandon Turner perform at The Handlebar's last show at the old mill.

A former auto dealership and auto-body shop morphs into The Handlebar's second location.

A bigger, better platform awaits bigger bands in the "new" Handlebar.

A handcrafted door, complete with flyers and posters advertising upcoming shows, opens to the magic of live music.
Photo by Jessica Tapp

Welcome to the club! The "Pedro" mural welcomes Handlebar patrons to the Stone Avenue location in Greenville.
Photo by Jessica Tapp

A pair of foam-made dice served as props for a Rolling Stones-themed benefit concert. They stayed a long time and ultimately disintegrated.
Photo by Jessica Tapp

Jennifer Nettles belts it out before rising to stardom with Sugarland.

the
Handlebar

304 E. Stone Ave.
GreenvilleSC 29609
(864) 233-6173

145

Jennifer
Nettles Band
w/ Jeffery Butts

Sat., October 13   9:00 pm

Ticket: $8.00
(General Admission. Tax included in price of ticket.)

The Handlebar's restaurant and bar sits on the other side of a wall from the venue's deliberately separated listening room.
Photo by Jessica Tapp

The folk-art-flavored work of Greenville artist Lu Wixon graces much of The Handlebar, including this mural over the main bar.
Photo by Jessica Tapp

The main entrance, complete with giant guitar and the de rigueur beer signs—and shows "where's outside?"
Photo by Jessica Tapp

Joan Baez at the Handlebar, October 5, 2003
Photo by Tanya Ackerman, courtesy of *Greenville News*

An old wooden sign from The Handlebar's first home at Mills Centre makes a spiffy table at the new location.
Photo by Jessica Tapp

Bartender Gary Bowling serves customers at the bar.
J. Scott Schrader Photography

A performance by the Drive-By Truckers on May 12, 2008.
Photo by Ed McDonald

Rebirth Brass Band
Photo by Ed McDonald

Dan Tyminski
Photo by Doug Anderson

The Zac Brown Band plays The Handlebar January 5, 2008.
Photo by Jason Williamson

Hundreds of artists, from Dr. John to Link Wray to Robert Earl Keen, have signed the giant guitar through the years.
Photo by Ken Osburn, *Greenville News*

room with a *pro bono* mediator. For an hour each session, I felt as if I'd been hauled into marriage counseling with somebody I'd never slept with. Eventually, of course, the series ended, and after our last session, the gentleman who had served as our mediator took me into the room alone and asked, "What did you think about all of this?"

Having been granted permission to speak freely in a Javert-free zone, I began an impassioned soliloquy in a rage that had been building up for years. I had waited all this time for anyone even *remotely* "official" to actually *hear* everything that I had endured all these years. I mean, you think this part of the story's dragging on, but put yourself in *my* shoes—I had gone into business for music, not for mediation, committees and cops.

"This guy's obsessed, you know that, right? He just won't stop." I tried to simmer down some, though I admit I was having a bit of fun. "What does he want, anyway? Really? He's never once said. We've spent countless hours—months!—on this crap. I spent how-much-time on that overblown committee? And how much *money* has the City spent on all these meetings and all these ridiculous police calls? We ourselves have spent *thousands* of dollars on sound baffling, with money we don't have, only for neighbors to complain that 'it didn't make any difference.' How would they know?"

In the end, Javert did manage to get City Council to rewrite the entire Noise Ordinance. Now, under the new regulations, it was illegal throughout Greenville to hold a backyard barbecue much later than the start of the evening news because people's voices exceed the lowered decibel limits.

Ultimately, the endless headache just sort of…went away. But not because Javert had "won" a new ordinance. No, we pretty much had Hurricane Katrina to thank for that. When remnants of the storm tore up the shingles on our roof, one of our partners gathered a crew to replace them. They also removed an old, useless ceiling fan, whose wide-open rooftop aperture had been acting all along as one big bull-horn.

◇
◇
◇

In spite of the occasional conflict here and there, The Handlebar was settling in through the middle of 2001. While I was trying to figure out what our new room could do and what the market would bear, we faced the customary summer doldrums. Memorial Day through the beginning of football season always marked the slowest time of year, not just in Greenville, where the weather creates too much competition, but also in the club business, when artists play festivals, state fairs and amphitheaters, or sheds, in industry parlance— the big-money gigs with huge crowds, big stages and much fancier catering.

While the Dave Alvin's Grand Reopening concert worked out fine, except for the part about our inability to sell alcohol, I took my first big risk financially and promotionally in our new room on a show that came only eight days after Dave Alvin's.

Richie Havens.

Richie was sixty-one years old at the time, a *bona fide* legend, a cultural icon. In 1969, he had blown away some four-hundred thousand people at Woodstock, with his historic performance of "Freedom." He had appeared on *The Ed Sullivan Show, The Tonight Show Starring Johnny Carson* and in movies and plays, namely with Bob Dylan and Richard Pryor.

Our new partners thought that I had pulled off a miracle when I told them that I had booked Richie.

"Richie fuckin' *Havens*?" one of them said. "You gotta be kiddin' me! How'd you get him?" (Of course, this was the same partner who, when he later saw Dave Mason of Traffic riff through a few classic hits during sound check on our stage, said: "What? This guy only does covers?" And the same partner who once threw me against a wall when he lost his temper.)

I just tried to explain to our new partner that you can get anything you want at the music-industry massacree . . . with the right amount of cash guaranteed to an agent and his artist.

I had worked for years with Richie's agent, Tim Drake, buying all manner of dates from him and his agency, which specialized primarily in folk artists. For Richie's concert, Tim and I negotiated what we both believed to be a good deal. His artist would get paid well, while our risk seemed reasonable, especially given the talent's marquee value and the novelty of our new location.

Only about two hundred fans showed up for Richie Havens. We lost a couple thousand dollars. Tim felt bad, but he and Richie still got paid. I felt worse. That's how the game was always played.

For the most part, though, I treaded lightly with my bookings, preferring to play it safe and relying on the old bullpen for proven powerhouses. Robert Earl Keen, the eminently popular Texas singer/songwriter who had long been a staple on the nationally syndicated John Boy & Billy radio show, came *this close* to selling out. It was especially gratifying to have him back—on a Tuesday!—and watch a room full of Shiner Bock-drenched fans scream out all the words to his "Merry Christmas from the Family" and, aptly, "The Road Goes On Forever (And The Party Never Ends)." The very next night, Leftover Salmon returned to Greenville, and Greenville returned in droves, selling out our three-week-old room.

Every now and then, one of my old contacts from the mill days would reappear. I had worked hard for the past six years to cultivate a network of reliable and trustworthy agents, and now they were popping up with a surprise or two—known in the industry as an "opportunity."

That's what happened after *O, Brother, Where Art Thou?* was released. The Coen Brothers film included a soundtrack that soon unleashed a national resurgence of bluegrass. The fervor bolstered our own regular bluegrass offerings and even our weekly Bluegrass Jam, a Tuesday night staple that had been on our calendar almost from the beginning. The film's collection of T. Bone Burnett-selected tunes instantly generated a Grammy buzz.

And that was when Randy Pitts called.

I smiled whenever I heard his distinctive voice. Randy was one of the best agents out there, working in Nashville for a boutique agency with a powerhouse roster. He was also one of the rare agents who had once been a promoter himself, the talent buyer for the storied Berkeley Freight & Salvage Coffeehouse. The Freight, which opened in California's counterculture paradise in 1968, held only about two hundred seats, but Randy booked some of the best acts in the business, including then-unknown Alison Krauss. So Randy knew the stresses of artist guarantees, and yet he could still balance the agency's requirements against the precarious and often perilous concerns of club owners.

Over the years, Randy had sold me tons of artists, including John Hartford, Guy Clark, bluegrass-guitar god Tony Rice, the Free Mexican Air Force's Peter Rowan, and the legendary Ralph Stanley, who was now on his way to picking up his own Grammy for "O Death" on the *O, Brother* album.

I knew that whenever Randy called good things would happen. We always shared a few laughs, traded music-industry gossip—Randy knew everybody inside Nashville and out—and we finally wrapped up a great booking opportunity. Our Old School conversations on the Old School telephone usually lasted only about fifteen minutes, with fewer than five of them spent on an actual contract negotiation. That's because Randy wasn't a salesman, he was a music fan, and he knew that he was talking with one of his own kind.

"I got a slam-dunk for you," he said.

"Coming from you, that means we'll have to spend a lot of money, but it also means that we might actually make a little, too."

"You've seen *O, Brother, Where Art Thou?*" he asked with his puckish chuckle.

"Oh, yeah, hasn't everybody?" I had a pretty good idea where he was going with this. "Okay, so, how is it that the agency you work for just so happens to represent almost every artist on that soundtrack?"

"How 'bout that, huh?" Then he launched into the story about how Burnett and one of the agency's clients, Gillian Welch, had plundered the roster for talent to make the album.

"You can't *possibly* be calling *me* to pimp out any of your *O, Brother* folks for my room. I mean, no way, they've got to be too big for us already."

He chuckled again. "Ever heard of Dan Tyminski? His band's a juggernaut."

Except for what I had heard on the soundtrack, I honestly didn't know much about Dan, though I *did* know that he had provided George Clooney's velvet voice in the movie's hit, "Man of Constant Sorrow." I definitely didn't know that Dan was also a monster guitarist and mandolin picker in Alison Krauss's band, Union Station.

"What about him? Them?"

"He's coming through and wants a date."

No freaking way. "Okay." I swallowed, trying to contain my excitement. "Tell me this. The band that he's got with him, they're not calling themselves the 'Soggy Bottom Boys,' are they?"

"Not officially, no, but everyone seems to be calling them that anyway." He laughed again. "You'll love him. He's one of the nicest, funniest guys you'll ever to work with. And he's probably going to want to play golf while he's there, he's a helluva golfer." He paused. "But it'll cost you." He quoted me a guarantee that the agency wanted for a show.

Oh, brother… "I guess there's no point in asking whether George Clooney comes with that price tag?"

Within a few minutes, I bit a financial bullet and booked the Dan Tyminski Band for a date in mid-July, a week after my forty-first birthday.

The show, predictably, sold out. Fans got treated to two hours of rockin' bluegrass. At the very end, Dan and the boys burst into "Man of Constant Sorrow." The crowd, as they say in the trades, went wild.

Meantime, while I reached out to the old network or waited for the good guys to call, I kept my eye on and continued bringing in those artists and genres I understood best.

A few weeks after Dan's sold-out appearance, we welcomed a pair of singer/songwriters from Atlanta. One of them, Kristen Hall, had captured my attention back when I lived in Florida, where I tuned in every morning to WMNF's three- or four-hour block of folk music. I had fallen hard for Kristen's husky voice, snappy lyrics and toe-tapping pop melodies and had booked her several times at the old mill, where I always asked her to play my favorite song, "Too Long Running." As soon as we reopened, I wanted Kristen back.

That summer, she returned to Greenville, bringing with her another young songwriter named Jennifer Nettles. At the time, Jennifer was also struggling to break out in Atlanta's crazy-competitive music scene.

Kristen seemed cranky that night, though I couldn't imagine why, and our dealings were brief and uncomfortable. At the same time, though, I couldn't get enough of her new sidekick. The first time I laid eyes on Jennifer Nettles, I thought I would explode. She was eyeball-jolting, slap-your-mama, knee-collapsing beautiful. To top it all off, her vibrant personality only complemented her strong voice and sultry stage presence.

The duo drew a respectable crowd, about a hundred and seventy fans at ten dollars a pop. Little did any of us know then that we had all just witnessed the beginnings of a band that would soon be called Sugarland.

While Kathy and I continued digging into our new location, all around us the music and touring business was experiencing convulsions that would change it forever. With construction, our new partners, day-to-day business concerns and ongoing attempts to cobble together a prudent but meaty calendar, I was too distracted to notice the temblors in the industry.

The year before, the nation's No. 2 radio broadcaster, Clear

Channel Communications, paid three-billion-plus dollars to purchase SFX, the leading concert promoter. That unleashed a torrent of mergers and consolidations that soon cascaded over the touring landscape, spilling over into the radio and recording industries as well. At the same time, another tsunami—the Digital Age—was about to sweep away the industry's longtime models.

One could argue that live music itself hadn't changed all that much in the last millennium or so. The violin, strung from the lute, is said to date back to the ninth century and the guitar to the twelfth. From caveman days on people sang songs to each other. Putting aside traveling minstrels who may have gotten paid during the Middle Ages, the rise of commercial *concert touring* is widely considered to have begun as far back as the 1960s. That's when Bill Graham transformed his San Francisco hippie-dance promotions into big-time national tours. By promoting the likes of the Rolling Stones and The Who in large venues, Graham earned millions and helped create a full-fledged industry.

Meanwhile technology happened. And with it, the turn of the latest century saw the launch of at least two new phenomena that started to shift at least a little of the power back to the artists and the fans, the very biological parents of rock 'n' roll. The two technological meteorites that slammed into the resource-gobbling planet of record labels, agents, global promoters and media conglomerates: Napster and the iPod.

Napster evolved from June 1999, before our eviction from the mill, through July 2001. The revolutionary website that traded in newfangled MP3 files almost immediately turned the music industry on its ear. Meanwhile, the iPod made music portable and even more accessible, on a scale that nobody could yet grasp.

But it was Napster that soon paved the way for artists to rethink their careers—from the way they distributed their work to the way they could unshackle themselves from major-label servitude. It's no secret that big-money record deals have historically pushed more artists than not into financial limbo rather than into fancy limos. Now, though, Napster allowed artists, especially the younger, hipper, more aggressive and more Internet-attuned ones, to exercise more control. They could leverage the powerful new cyber-distribution tool to access and win more and more fans, those millions of kids out there who were sharing and stealing millions of songs. Those same kids then spread the word about all these great new tunes they were discovering online. And while Napster did fire the first torpedo into the torpid recording industry, it was the artists using the hot prod-uct-delivery system who realized that they could make even more money the old-fashioned way: touring. Get your music out to the world, on your own schedule, and your newfound fans will flock to see you play all the songs they already know. In short, artists could now pull off their own classic capitalist maneuver—cut out a few power-wielding, money-hungry middlemen and keep the change. The same model, incidentally, though analog, had worked just fine for the Grateful Dead, Allman Bros. and J. Geils Band, all of whom earned more money from the road than they did from record sales. The Dead had always encouraged fans to tape concerts and swap bootlegs, in part to expand their fan base, while the band also sold mountains of merchandise on their long, strange trip.

I first experienced Napster and the emerging digital paradigm soon after we reopened. To be sure, I had heard of the song-swapping site, but I had no idea how it worked or what good it could do me. I mean, I was still getting used to the idea of the Internet itself and to email. I was what you'd call Old School. I worked the phones, sent offers to agents via the archaic facsimile machine and even occasion-ally mailed letters with actual stamps to people.

See, way back at the mill, I needed to build relationships with those all-powerful agents. Most of them worked in fancy offices in San Francisco's Bay Area, New York, Los Angeles, Chicago and Nashville. They controlled the careers and fates of countless artists, the very people I needed to attract customers who would, hopefully, fill our cash registers. My job entailed sending out feelers to or, just as often, fielding calls and emails from agents seeking "avails"—industry lingo for routing dates that his particular artist would be available in our market. On my booking calendar, then, I would hold various avails for an agent, often giving him three, four or even five dates, until he figured out his band's routing and collected the biggest guarantees from each promoter along the way. Once the agent secured his tour deals, he called the promoters to confirm the shows, and tickets went on sale to the fans. The whole process is messy and mildly complicated, riddled with unwritten and arcane rules—all of them established by and thus benefitting the agencies. Any promoter who somehow violated a hold, double-booked a date or committed any other such calendar mishap heard post-haste from the aggrieved agency's copraphiliac, whose withering telephonic barrage included: "You'll never do business with us again, you slimy, untrustworthy sonofabitch!" So, yes, it is on this cobbled system, which often works against the promoter's best interests, that all-important "relationships" in the music business are built.

By the time we reopened, I had established a pretty solid Rolodex. (Remember those?)

One summer afternoon, I got a call from Scott Clayton.

Scott was one of those agents for whom I would hold an entire month's worth of dates for one of his artists if he needed that much flexibility. He and I had contracted any number of bands together through the years. I had always considered him one of the best agents in the country, even though I didn't learn until much later that he was also a homeboy, a native of nearby Spartanburg. Now, he worked for Creative Artists Agency, one of the biggest talent and sports agencies on the planet. CAA's massive roster included Stephen Spielberg, Stevie Wonder, Bon Jovi and hundreds more. Scott worked with smaller acts in CAA's Nashville office, where he was quickly building a reputation for finding young artists and developing them into Big Names. Scott had also once worked for Nashville's Progressive Global Agency, founded the same year that we opened, with a roster that included Widespread Panic and R.E.M. The guarantees he solicited were almost always reasonable and fair and, so, likely lucrative or at least worth the risk. Besides all that, he was always fun to talk to.

"I've got a new guy you should be interested in," he said.

I already knew by then that we would likely lose money on a couple of upcoming shows, including Richie Havens and some other chancy bookings. Which meant that I had to hold my horses, rein in my excitement about what we could get away with, so I told him: "Sorry, can't afford it."

He wasn't fazed. He had always been one of the few agents out there who sympathized with promoters and cared whether a club took a haircut on one of his artists. "Don't worry about it. We'll work out a low-risk deal that'll work for everyone."

Unh-hunh. I had heard that pitch before. Through my skittish pause, he continued:

"Trust me, this guy's going to take off."

Heard that one, too. Agents earn their ten- or fifteen-percent commissions selling their clients, trumpeting their hot new artists as the next Sting, the next Tom Petty, the next Dylan. Although Scott had never been the usual used-car-salesman agent—at least, not with me, anyway—he nevertheless believed in his product. He handpicked young rock 'n' rollers for a place on CAA's roster; his tested instincts told him that their talent would take them places, with his help. At the same time, Scott knew that promoters, especially small fry like The Handlebar, were crucial to developing his baby bands' careers. No venues, no artists, and vice versa.

Since I was speaking with Scott Clayton, I relented. "Okay, I'm listening. But, really, how is it that anybody has ever even heard of your guy, especially around *here*?" It helped, of course, that he knew exactly what "around *here*" meant.

"Napster. It's that simple. This kid's throwing his stuff all over Napster, and everybody's downloading it."

"But wait a second, bud. Napster's free, and now you're telling me that your guy is *giving* his music away?"

He chuckled, in that visionary way of his, as if to say: Oh, Grasshopper, the things you must learn in this sprawling, shiny, revolutionary Digital Age. "That's where things are going. He puts his songs up on Napster, and the next thing you know, he plays a new town and sells a place out, first time in."

All this sounded counterintuitive at best, speculative at least. "But if his music is free, how is he—and, by extension, how are *you*—supposed to make any money?"

"Ticket revenues. The artist makes all his money at the gate, not so much on album sales anymore, more and more on live shows, touring. That's how things look like they're moving."

"I don't know, man—"

"I'll tell you what. Send me an offer with a low-ball guarantee. It's no band, just him, solo/acoustic, so you won't have lot of extra expenses, no hospitality rider to speak of and hardly anything in the way of tech: just a microphone and a stage monitor, that's about it."

The moment he said "acoustic," I smiled to myself: Yay! No bullshit call to the cops from our buddy nearby. Maybe a few car doors closing when fans returned to the busy parking lot after the show at around eleven or so, but not enough "noise" for another Javert broadside.

"…And the show will go great, I promise you, so we'll book him again a few months later. I guarantee that you'll pack out your room, if not the first show, then definitely the second time in."

Easy for you to say, big guy. A broken promise can be forgotten or forgiven, but a bad bet can leave lasting dismay. Besides, I told Scott, this ain't *your* bet. *You* don't have to put *your* wallet where *my* venue is.

He told me what kind of deal he wanted, a minimal guarantee that sounded fairly nonthreatening and reasonably do-able. So I sent him an offer—the one he wanted. He called back a week or so later to confirm the show for May 31, our eighth one in our new room and barely three weeks after our reopening.

When the twenty-three-year-old Digicrat/songwriter pulled into our load-in area, everything I thought I knew about the music business suddenly made no sense. How could an unknown artist already afford to rent a half-million-dollar tour bus? He hadn't even released his first album yet. His record label was something of an upstart, too, making a name for itself by making names for artists who had yet to make a name for themselves. In other words, the label couldn't possibly have plied him with that much tour-support cash.

While I watched the young man's crowd line up outside our doors, I stepped into the concert hall for the sound check. Just a kid alone onstage with his guitar. I wanted to see for myself why he was such a big deal. Ever since we had announced his appearance, the phones started ringing. Fans called in droves to order tickets. What in the world *was* this? Who *were* these people? I had never even heard this guy's music. I didn't own an iPod, and nobody had ever mailed us an advance copy of the debut EP. What I saw onstage that afternoon was a lean, good-looking young man who played guitar with the effortless proficiency of a veteran bluesman. His tenor ran deep and smooth, like Cuban rum. His lyrics, catchy and commercial, spoke straight to his swelling crowd: swooning teenaged girls, swaggering frat boys and the occasional soccer mom. Really, who *were* these people? I stood at the merchandise booth, where I also glanced over at—okay, coveted—a blue sweatshirt that sported a logo as striking as it was simple. The front of the navy hoodie featured a single, iconic image: a computer-cursor pointer, the puffy right-hand forefinger and thumb extended, as in Click. To Listen.

A few hours later, an astonishing two hundred and thirty-plus fans went wild in our Listening Room—nearly half our capacity, yet more people than we had seen for our Grand Reopening or for the legendary Richie Havens. These kids, it turned out, weren't Handlebar fans at all. They were high school drama queens and prom kings who sang all the words to all the songs that they had downloaded off Napster.

A week later, the Aware Records label released *Room For Squares*, but that night at The Handlebar virtually everyone either already owned the album or at least some digital pieces of it. So when he launched into "Your Body Is A Wonderland," the pretty girls giggled and the boys squirmed, and when he sang "No Such Thing," they all screamed along, as if running through the halls of their high schools.

After his show, the young troubadour sat on the edge of our stage and talked a couple of hours through a snaking line of star-struck kids. He even indulged one gawky worshipper with a mini-lesson on guitar chords and keys and other music arcana. I joined the end of the line, to thank him for a great show and the great numbers, especially considering his first time in the room and in the market. When the room emptied, he walked with me over to the merch booth, where he handed me one of those badass hoodies. I still wear it.

A year and a half after his second—and last—Handlebar show, John Mayer won his first Grammy Award. Better than that, I was told that, one night, during an arena show in Nashville, he mentioned The Handlebar by name to some sixteen-thousand fans; you can't buy advertising like that.

The very next night, I watched the same story about Napster's nascent power unfold, only this time in an entirely different way.

Adrian Legg had played for us numerous times back at the old mill. He always put on an easy show—simple hospitality and tech riders. Adrian was also great to be around. His martini-dry British wit amplified his intellect, as sharp and spontaneous as his brilliant jazz-guitar work.

In those days, the diminutive musician was enjoying a good run. He had a regular series on National Public Radio; his American commentary brimmed with hysterical perspectives. He had also been busy collecting accolades. Readers of the United Kingdom's *Gui-*

tarist magazine had named him Guitarist of the Decade for 1984 to 1994. *Guitar Player's* readers voted him Best Acoustic Fingerstylist four years in a row in the mid-'90s. Ex-Deep Purple guitar god Joe Satriani had called Adrian "simply the best acoustic guitar player I've ever seen."

But while Adrian may have been an instrumental wizard, he still used an Old School compass to navigate the industry's shifting land-scape.

After his sound check, Adrian paced around outside our con-cert hall. He rubbed his wrists, looking a bit pained. He was dressed entirely in black, so even his gnomish grin couldn't hide his quiet grimness.

"Are you okay?" I asked. "Can I get you anything?"

"Just a little carpal tunnel"—a bit like a surgeon saying, *No wor-ries, just losing my eyesight.* He said he was waiting on his wife to join him for dinner in our restaurant. "How are ticket sales looking?"

"Pretty light, I'm afraid, no more than about fifty pre-sales."

He grimaced. "Well, hopefully, we'll have plenty of walkup."

"Y'know, it's an interesting thing…We just had John Mayer here last night, and he did more than two hundred paid."

"Don't know him." He shook his head. I could see his brain kick into gear, as quick and supple as the fingers that earned his living. He seemed to be racing through a series of calculations. "Hmm. How do you figure?"

"Well, see, that's what surprised me, too. Everyone knew him before he even walked through the door…Napster—"

"Now, that's the bloody end of us all." His shoulders rounded, hackles raised. "If Napster and the like aren't the beginning of piracy, this entire file-sharing business is the beginning of the end of music that people will pay for." He shook his head a bit more, his gray-matter machine churning even harder under that balding pate and behind those geeky black glasses. "Once the music's devalued, given away, even stolen, where's the livelihood in *that*? How will it be possible for any artist to earn a living then?"

"Well, I think that's the whole point, see? A guy like John Mayer gives away his music, and all these kids show up at his shows." I pointed toward the empty concert hall. The doors were papered with posters, including his: the black-clad artist standing next to a dangling noose and holding a guitar. "Most of the ticket revenue from last night? That's *bank*, that's *his* money, not some record label's. He's going to make it all on touring."

He looked resigned.

"I mean, look," I said. "He made almost three times more than you'll probably earn tonight, even though your ticket's two dollars higher. And that's only because, imagine if everyone out there"—I waved toward the pretty June weather—"what if everyone knew all your tunes?"

That night, Adrian drew about ninety ticket buyers.

For the first time in history—in my life, anyway—technology was propelling art, rather than the other way around. Edison's tinfoil phonograph propelled music and Johannes Gutenberg's printing press did wonders for books. Now, the Internet was wreaking havoc on *homo sapiens'* eternally entrenched analog existence.

I still didn't have the foggiest notion how to harness any of it.

Neither was I prepared for what happened on that sparkling Tuesday morning in 2001.

Nobody was.

8

When that singular September morning saw a new gash rip through history, Kathy and I were still asleep. One of our partners called to wake us up. "Turn on your TV," he told us, "right now. You'll never believe what just happened."

For much of the day, we stayed in our pajamas, glued to the television. Along with everyone else, we couldn't wrap our heads around the all-encompassing horror. The enormity of it all left little room for thought about anything else.

But while the hours dragged us into shock, we eventually had to confront an even more terrifying future. What would happen next? What *could* happen next?

Beyond our elemental understanding that we weren't facing some garden-variety snow- or ice storm that day, we still faced a similar uncertainty. We had shows booked that week. What would we do about them? What *could* we do about them?

From the earliest days of The Handlebar, Tuesday nights had always given us the rare chance to enjoy something that small businesses don't usually get: routine. Tuesdays meant friends and home-grown bluegrass and the Swing Dance. Gene Dillard, a witty and smart special-education teacher who also played a mean standup bass, had been the core of our Bluegrass Jam. Gene helped round up pickers, amateurs and a few ringers, who brought in their guitars, banjos, mandolins and fiddles, as well as another doghouse bass or two and the occasional harmonica and Dobro, the guitar whose shiny metallic resonator in the middle looked like a hubcap. Fans joined along, singing down-home gems, playing spoons, occasionally clogging and always taking in the fellowship that filled our bar. Meanwhile, in the Listening Room, Paul Hoke and his wife, Ansley, ran the weekly Swing Dance. They taught clean-cut kids, including some exotic and subversive Bob Jones University escapees, how to do the Lindy Hop and the Charleston. Years after I had proclaimed to Paul, "Swing is dead," big crowds danced to CDs that played Big Band, R&B and oldies-rock.

Tuesdays always brought people together, and *that* tragic Tuesday was no different. Some people may have shown up that night because they knew that life had to go on. Others might have considered it their patriotic duty to go out and spend money and keep America running. Most, though, it seemed, just wanted to be with other people, to gather round the TVs in the bar in hopes of assuaging the tragedy by sharing it.

While eight fifty-six that morning had now become this generation's JFK-assassination and Pearl Harbor moments, the night slipped into increasing anxiety about the days ahead.

For us, signed contracts loomed for two months' worth of concerts, from Commander Cody & His Lost Planet Airmen, best known for their 1972 hit, "Hot Rod Lincoln," through Gillian Welch and David Rawlings, best known for playing in the dark.

Would any of these shows be canceled? What would the artists and their agents do—or expect from us and benumbed fans? Would we really have to stage concerts that people might *not feel like seeing*?

It so happened that two of the shows immediately following 9/11 came from a San Francisco-based agency that represented several fine blues and roots artists: John Lee Hooker, Robert Cray Band, Beausoleil and the two performers I had booked for that week, Marcia Ball on September 12 and David Lindley for the following Friday.

In booking Marcia Ball, I had deliberately violated Livingston Taylor's first commandment about buying talent as a fan—as I had lots of times before and would continue to do; I was a purist and, despite the pitfalls, would remain one. I had always been a Marcia Ball devotee. I'd thrown Mardi Gras beads in New Orleans' Maple Leaf tavern while watching her eternally long legs kick along with her bayou-blues keyboard. I'd seen her in several states, from the state of Massachusetts to a state of drunken euphoria.

David Lindley was another favorite, too, dating from way back when Horizon Records' Gene Berger had booked him to play the old mill when the space wasn't even ready to open yet. Gene was no longer promoting shows in town, but he helped us spread the word about Lindley, a musician's musician who had always been one of the greatest instrumentalists around. Lindley's probably most famous for his falsetto voice and distinctive guitar sound on Jackson Browne's classic "Stay," but he'd also collaborated with iconoclasts Ry Cooder and Warren Zevon. For our show, Lindley was bringing along Sheryl Crow's insanely talented drummer, Wally Ingram.

Even before 9/11, Kathy and I feared that neither of these shows would do well. As our usually dismal summer season was wrapping up, we couldn't figure out why these hot autumn shows weren't selling. We had mustered as much promotion as we knew how, but it still appeared inevitable that we would lose money, at least on one of them. Interestingly, I had offered the same amount of money for each act, tendering those guarantees on the good-faith assumption that we would have little trouble drawing enough ticket buyers to cover those fees. Both performers had drawn well at the mill, so we needed less than half that old capacity.

You can never know, until you see advance sales so sluggish and hear no buzz.

As early as August, I had started emailing the agent—we'll call him Ron. From time to time, I sent him an alert about the sorry state of ticket sales. His responses essentially said: *Gee, hate to hear that, too bad. Please send the required fifty-percent deposit.* In other words, rather than helping us find some creative solutions to promote our way out of potential pecuniary pain, he instead demanded money. We owed the agency the customary fifty-percent deposit, due one month out. The agency wanted the cash *now*—money that simply wasn't there from ticket sales that weren't there, either.

Sure, it was true that *I* was the one who had made the offers. Nobody, as they *really do* say in the trade, had stuck a gun to my head forcing me to guarantee the artists "so much" money.

"*You* were the one who wanted those shows," Ron said, using the shopworn chestnut that agents always used to happily and squarely place the blame on incompetent promoters, the foolish gamblers who make the bad bets.

Still, though, I held out some small hope that Ron or, perhaps, the agency would consider giving us a hand if those shows went south. Stuff like that happened. Rarely.

Predictably, we lost money on both shows.

The following Monday, I pleaded with Ron: "Can't we get a reduction on these or, really, to be fair, at least on Marcia? I mean, c'mon, the day after *Nine-Eleven*! Seriously, doesn't anybody at the agency have a heart, a little compassion? Good lord, nobody wanted—"

"Our artists were there, ready to play. They fulfilled their end of the contract."

"And I fulfilled ours."

"Nobody said you didn't."

"But . . . " I might as well have been trying to fly a kite on the moon.

Soon, Ron sent an email saying, in essence, that he was sorry, but those were the breaks, kid, tough luck. The agency's no-reduction, you-bought-it/you-eat-it policy was part of the agency's "corporate culture," he wrote. In essence, he was telling me: We did our job, and as a promoter, you should have done yours.

Sure, I could tell Ron and the agency that theaters in the Bay Area don't do much business after an earthquake or that some films just play to lighter-than-expected crowds—temblor or terrorist attack notwithstanding. I could tell the agency that promoters for the most part don't intentionally neglect their promotional efforts just to lose money, though too many agents through the years have made that perverse insinuation. Regardless, nobody there would care.

Through the rest of that sad September, we lost money on more than half of our concerts. Only Commander Cody gave us a little reduction. I was the one, after all, who had *wanted* those shows. Apparently, the agents *needed* those shows and the money that we paid their artists, but many of them made it clear that they didn't need The Handlebar.

Back when I was a young newspaperman, brimming with big ambitions and the self-confidence of an adolescent, I could have been the inspiration for the bumper sticker: "Hire A Teenager While He Still Knows Everything!" In my newsroom days, I often considered the Assistant City Editor an idiot, the Managing Editor a moron and the bureau chief a mindless stooge whose only job was to kiss hierarchical ass. All that changed as soon as I opened my own business. Now, *I* was the Idiot-in-Charge. What I soon learned was that my onetime superiors were no more incompetent fops than I was an inevitable Pulitzer Prize winner. Yes, I realized pretty damned fast that some of their decisions were likely based on corporate Darwinism, especially those jump-shot judgment calls that seemed incomprehensible or senseless to me at the time. Only the shrewd survived. Now *I* had to be the one who had to be astute. *I* was the new Bozo helping to run the circus.

Throughout my newspaper days, despite my less-than-appreciative attitude toward my ink-stained superiors, I was still blessed with some valuable mentors. But when I wandered haplessly into the cutthroat music industry, I found that a replacement counselor just wasn't there.

Sure, the marketplace is chock full of small-business role models, advisors, consultants and the like, but in the isolated and insulated world of talent-buying, a knowledgeable and sympathetic mentor was about as easy to find as a virgin on an aircraft carrier. It takes a true music-industry insider to understand and convey the ins-and-outs of contract negotiations and filling a calendar; the esoteric mechanics of a process that operates with "rules" one day and different protocols for *other* players the next; and what "relationships" really mean in an industry that seems to just give lip service to them. Anyone who has any experience or familiarity with all those issues, as well as the patience to help somebody figure them out, isn't typically the kind of mentor you would meet a local Rotary Club.

And yet, I was blessed again. Not long after we opened, I fell in with a guide, even though he happened to be an agent.

I met Sean LaRoche the same way that I had met virtually every broker in the business: over the phone.

LaRoche grew up in Manhattan, back when the world was black 'n' white, men wore fedoras and youngsters "rebelled" by cohabitating in cold-water flats. He was a man of the Fifties who still had that easygoing, Ike-era optimism, which apparently had never flagged despite his years working in an industry that ceaselessly chewed away at it. He had the heart of an artist, and I think he even saw himself as a remnant of that whole Beats scene; he often alluded to Ginsberg and Kerouac and the rest, and it wouldn't surprise me if he had spent some time with them.

Sean got his start in the music business after dropping out of Yale. In the Sixties, he was road manager for country star Roger Miller, and in the Seventies, he joined Frank Barsalona's Premier Talent agency.

In 1964, Barsalona opened the shop that industry veterans credit with launching rock 'n' roll touring in America. Premier created the first U.S. tours for the Beatles, Stones and Yardbirds. LaRoche, back home in New York and working for Barsalona, handled the likes of Led Zeppelin and The Who.

Over time, Sean's arena-rock history gave way to an abiding love for solo singer/songwriters. He tended to gravitate toward the female ones. And he seemed to know damn near everybody in the folk world, from personal acquaintance or from a professional relationship or from his passion for their art. He knew Dar Williams and Mary Gauthier and Lucy Kaplansky. He was hip to Vance Gilbert, Ellis Paul and John Gorka. He knew about Jennifer Nettles while she was struggling as a singer/songwriter at Atlanta's Eddie's Attic, long before anybody, including Jennifer, knew about Sugarland.

Those who worked with Sean will tell you two things: When he believed in an artist and her potential, he threw himself into her career the way a linebacker throws himself at a quarterback—all bets were off until he made a score, and then another score, and another. Secondly, Sean could spend more time talking on the phone than any agent alive. Friends and colleagues often joked that his telephone bill *had* to exceed the meager commissions he earned from booking these off-the-mainstream performers. Little wonder that he talked often about how broke he was.

Sean and I spent hours on the phone.

Whenever he called, I smiled as soon as I heard his voice, as recognizable as my own Dad's. Sean sounded like your favorite teddy bear, if your favorite teddy bear could talk—y'know, the one with the sewn-on arm, mismatched button eyes and scruffy fuzz.

He always started his calls the same way, and he often playfully tossed around the lingo of some slick Hollywood rainmaker.

"Jeter, LaRoche."

"LaRoche, y'old bastard, who are you calling about today to rip me off, hmm?"

"Babe. You gotta hear this chick, she's the real deal."

"Uh-huh. And she's different from your last 'real deal' . . . how?"

"Well, she just played Strawberry Fest, you know, that huge hippie-folkie deal out in California, and they're already screaming to have her back. I gotta tell you, she's raw, I mean it, but she's really got the stuff, man, I'm telling you. You might want to slice your veins open when you hear her, but give her a chance, babe, just one listen, and you'll see what I mean."

Of course, most of what Sean said could apply to every singer/ songwriter he had fallen in love with. As soon as he believed in an artist, he could wax biblically about her talent, her charisma and her career potential.

"Hey, Sean, you got a minute?"

"For you, all day." He chuckled that warm, cigarette-seared chuckle. "C'mon, Jeter, it's LaRoche you're talking to."

"Sean, I swear to god, you wouldn't believe what this sonofabitch just told me today." Thus began my customary rant. He would listen and occasionally chortle, as if I were telling the world's worldliest man something he had never heard. "This rat bastard just said to me, 'You *will not* call this agency or email this agency or speak to anyone in this agency unless we call you first with our artists' avails. You don't *buy* dates from us, we *sell* dates to you. Is that clear?' Can you *believe* that shit, Sean? I mean, seriously, first of all, how fucking patronizing is *that*? And, secondly, how does that tack even remotely serve the artists on their roster, *their* clients?"

"Lemme guess," whereupon he named the very agent who had just enlightened me about How Things Worked.

"How'd you know who I was talking about?"

"Because the same guy made another one of my promoters cry once." He sighed.

"You're kidding, right?"

"No, and I'll tell you . . . " Then he named a bunch of big shots, movers, shakers, moguls and mopes, somehow connecting all of us, one way or another, through just a few degrees of separation. He made the whole industry sound like one big happy family, and in Sean's world, every last one of us was a contributing member. That's because, I suppose, he *wanted* things that way. "It ain't brain surgery and it ain't rocket science, right?"

"Which is a damn good thing, my friend, because you were the one who taught me that if this *was* rocket science or brain surgery, we'd both have lobotomies in outer space by now."

"Seriously, take a listen to this gal. I'll send you her new record." A package would arrive in a day or so, along with a postcard whose black-Sharpie inscription always read in his illegible scrawl: Love ya, Sean.

"Okay, LaRoche, since it's coming from you, I'll listen, even though you know I don't listen to CDs anymore and haven't since the first time I listened all the way through Eddie From Ohio's first record."

For the next few minutes, then, we talked about EFO, a band that he went on to represent for a while. And after another fifteen minutes or so of kvetching and gossiping, we again went back to business.

"Jeter, just give her a shot, okay? Let her play some opening slot, I get that, and maybe throw her a hundred bucks, and maybe even a little bonus if you get a crowd. Then, after you see her, tell me, just tell me that you didn't go crazy for her and want to bring her back—fast. And next time for the big dough."

That's how we did many of our deals with his artists. No contracts, no deposits, no risks. Just a telephonic handshake.

Sean helped build the careers of Ani DiFranco, Jerry Jeff Walker, Martin Sexton and many others.

Sean LaRoche was as real and as genuine as the artists he represented; otherwise he likely wouldn't represent them. If he believed in you and what you were trying to do, he wanted to be part of the solution, not part of the problem—even if you were a promoter. At one point, he went so far as to try and help me find a literary agent for a novel I had recently written. He called his longtime friend, Malachy McCourt, the brother of *Angela's Ashes* author Frank McCourt. Nothing ever happened with that novel. But because of his generosity, a lot of singer/songwriters who still play today owe some of their livelihoods to Sean's early nurturing.

One day, I called him up just to ask how he was doing. His health was faltering. He had lived hard, smoked all his life, moved around a lot. Not long before, he had relocated to Florida to be closer to his daughter.

"Where are you?" I asked.

"In Florida."

"I know that, goofball."

"I'm out on the patio. They don't let you smoke in hospice."

Sean died of esophageal cancer a few days later in Ocala. He was only seventy-one years old.

Tim Drake, from whom I had bought the Richie Havens date and with whom Sean had formed the short-lived Drake & LaRoche agency, said of Sean in one obituary: "He's a great soul. He'd spend so much time talking with buyers and artists, artists who weren't even on our roster, to help them out. That was his greatest passion, to help singer/songwriters." In another obit, Tim said: "I visited him a couple of weeks ago, and there he was, practically on his deathbed, still wrapping up a festival deal for a friend he believed in. That was Sean."

Indeed.

The late, great gonzo journalist, Hunter S. Thompson, once said: "The music business is a cruel and shallow money trench, a long plastic hallway where thieves and pimps run free, and good men die like dogs. There's also a negative side."

Sean was one of the few who defied all that. And I never once told him how profoundly he and his friendship had helped me learn to navigate the cruel and shallow money trench. He was neither thief nor pimp, he was just a good man who died doing what he loved to do—believing as much in his artists as in what he tried to do for them. At the same time, he never wanted to hurt anybody who also wanted to help—namely his buyers, with whom he saw shared risk and love for the art. I still believe that that's why we clicked and remained as close as we did.

I never met Sean, never once saw him in person. The only picture that I've ever seen of him is blurry. Still, I loved LaRoche, and I still miss him. Some days, I just want to pick up the phone and spend an hour or so with him.

"Babe," I'd say, "you ain't never gonna *believe* this shit…"

As a would-be artist myself, with a bushel of bad novels under my belt and dreams of my own blockbuster showing up on *Oprah!,* I clung to the fatal notion that Art and Commerce simply *had* to be *simpatico.* I told myself, over the course of some twenty years and countless rejection slips, that one day a major publishing house would eventually "buy" one of my books. My work had artistic value! Okay, it might not make anyone a zillion dollars, but still…!

It didn't take long for me to see that just as every Pat Conroy and Tom Clancy wannabe out there dreamed of a book deal, the world was equally loaded with Coldplay and Corey Smith wannabes—all of them, as The Boss once said, hustling for the record machine.

Now, though, as The Handlebar's talent buyer, I had become a *de facto* publisher. I was the one who doled out only so many opportunities to those artists whom I believed would, yes, make us money. Talent, of course, meant a lot, but for our needs, it didn't always mean coin. In a nutshell, my job entailed trying to figure out who was worth what when.

The big question has always been and always will be: How was I supposed to do that? How is any small-venue talent buyer supposed to decide who will be a good investment, who might go on to stardom? And who, finally, is worth the risk? Because when the night ends, it's the promoter who makes those fateful gambles.

By now, The Handlebar was receiving thousands of queries every month for artists to play our room. The inquiries came in from all over, from across the street and around the world, from local bands and big-time booking agents, and from everyone in between. The solicitations arrived by email, phone, fax, snail-mail and the occasional walk-in: an excited dad waving around his kid's band's killer press kit with their new EP, or the earnest bass player telling us how his band was rockin' the next town over. Soon, we were getting more than three thousand inquiries every year, but our calendar could accommodate roughly ten percent of them. In other words, we promoted an average of a hundred and twenty shows annually. An evening's bill typically included one headliner and two opening acts, so we could stage fewer than four hundred artists a year.

That made for a lot of rejections. For the most part, talent agencies either didn't care that I passed on one of their artists, or the agents saved me the trouble: They simply didn't call or email with any of their touring avails, despite how much I was willing to offer or how many fans in my market wanted to see their bands. So it fell to the local and regional bands to take my rejections or, most often, my neglect the hardest.

If I happened to be in the office when one of them called to get a gig, the conversations generally went this way:

"Dude, who's the booker there?" the hopeful headliner asked.

"You're talking to him, I'm the talent buyer for The Handlebar."

"Right on. Okay, I got this band that'll pack your place."

" 'Zat so?" We had just promoted Nils Lofgren, *Rolling Stone* magazine's No. Four guitarist of all-time and the wizard of Springsteen's E-Street Band, and *he* couldn't pack our place, but, whatever. . .

"We rock."

"I see." Cue here: biting my lip and running my fingers through my thinning hair. "So, um, what's the name of your kickass band?"

"The Dust Bunnies."

"Awesome. What do you guys sound like?"

"Man, our music's just too hard to describe. We just started a few months ago, but we're giving Nickelback and The Ramones a run for their money. Oh, and we do a lot of covers."

If that was, in fact, a faithful description of the Bunnies' product, I wouldn't be able to handle much more of this conversation before my head exploded. "Hmm, wow, that's, um, *that's* original." Long pause, drum fingers on desk. "Do you guys have a CD out?"

"We're working on one, y'know? We're, like, in the drummer's studio right now, but the guitar player just broke up with his girl-friend."

Natch. "You said you guys live…where?"

"Gaffney." He named the hamlet about forty-five minutes away, under the world-renowned Peachoid, the water tower that resembles a giant peach but has always looked to me more like a huge butt that's mooning God.

"Any of you guys…um, have *you* ever been here before?"

"No, man."

A signal to hang up now. "Have you been to our website, where we have this whole long page about our booking policies?"

"What's your website address?"

Bite lip one last time, before deciding that it might not be worth hurting myself over this. "You *do* know that our capacity's about five hundred, right? Well, that's a pretty big space to fill." Let's see, how can I let this nice kid down gently? "Just so I'm following you, y'all don't have a CD out yet, and I guess the Dust Bunnies aren't getting any radio play in the market?"

"Five hundred, you said? That might be a little small for us, to be honest."

I was now fresh out of reasonable responses. Instead, I was think-ing about how I could make this same kind of pitch to a publisher or literary agent, assuming that I would ever get one on the phone—which I wouldn't. But still, I could hear myself making a classic pitch for one of my books: Yo, homes, I just wrote this kick-ass novel that *kills*, right? It's kind of like what would happen if Hemingway rewrote *Harry Potter*.

One afternoon, though, I actually *did* attempt to explain how to get your first gig. My friend, Mike, had dropped by. He owned the nearby bicycle shop, which I patronized, and he frequently came in to buy tickets. On this particular day, he asked if I could spare a few minutes to talk about his son's band.

Happy to accommodate him, *but just him*, I smiled and said, "Sure," even though I said to myself: Uh-oh, I have to lead yet another neophyte into the shadowy underbelly of show business.

"My son's band really is good," he told me, "so I wanted to ask your advice." He seemed nervous, as if he were applying for a job in Microsoft's executive suite—awfully generous of him to think so highly of us, but still. "I was wondering if maybe you could tell me or tell him or maybe tell both of us about what it takes, what these guys need to do to make it, to get a show here, that sort of thing."

"How much time you got?"

"Plenty. My guys have everything under control at the shop, so as much time as you can afford, I guess."

I folded my hands together. "Listen, Mike, I'll bet your kid's an amazing talent. But lemme tell you." He seemed poised to hear me tell him where *X* marked the spot on the industry's treasure map. "Let's put it this way: I go to your store and drop five, six grand on a *serious* racing bike. Of course, you and I both know that I'm in okay shape, but there I am, standing in the middle of your store, and I say, 'Man, this thing is badass! Now, do you have a few minutes to tell me how to win the Tour de France?' "

With so many queries, it was simply impossible to take as much time as all that to explain *any* rejection. Some band guys took it well: "Oh, don't worry, man, you'll be seeing us one day," while at least one said, before hanging up on me: "You're an asshole."

Emails were a lot easier, and though they filled—and refilled—our Inbox, they all came with a Delete button.

"To Whom It May Concern:"

"Booker:"

"Hey,"

"Dear _____"

And the grand-prize query came as a *text message* to our email address: "How can someone perform at the bar?"

One day, an anxious soccer mom walked in with a brand-new CD from her son's band. She asked if I could please listen to it. As I had once told my friend, Sean LaRoche, I hadn't listened to much of a CD, let alone listened to an entire one, since Eddie From Ohio's 1993 album. By that time, I had already understood that even if I fell in love with a band's music, as I had with EFO's *Actually Not*, how could I sell it to my market, where too few people had likely ever heard it? At any rate, a couple of weeks later, the hopeful mom called back.

"Hi, remember me? I dropped off my son's CD with you, and I just hope you got a chance to listen to it."

"Yes, ma'am, it's great. I'm sure you're really proud."

"Wow! Cool!" I could almost see her counting ticket receipts for her son's college fund. "Oh, and I need it back."

"You mean, um, the CD? Really?" Yikes. "Oh, sure, we'll have a look around, but that could take awhile 'cause we've got several hundred CDs here."

"That'd be great," she said. "It's the only copy we have."

If only booking bands were like buying groceries: I walk into the store and head over to Aisle 7, where the entire left side displays four or five shelves of cereals. As a typical American consumer, I would zero in on the brand, as much the type, of breakfast I want, from Cap'n Crunch® to Kellogg's Raisin Bran®. A store may stock more than three hundred brands of cereal, but the live-music "product" touring the country and pouring out of local garages numbers well into the intergalactic.

So, again: How *does* a small club talent buyer go about buying talent for his small club?

Obviously, learning the process never ends, especially in a pop-culture world that shifts in minutes and in an industry that continues to convulse. Once upon a time, music was recorded on a wax cylinder, and anyone who wanted to hire a band just had to pick up a phone. Nowadays, the whole world's gone digital, and the technological dust may never settle.

When we first opened, I bought talent the old-fashioned way: calling agents or actual band members and negotiating a deal that sometimes meant sending an offer via one of those quaint facsimile machines. The offers that I made in those days generally resulted from a method as thoughtful and scientific as one used to play a slot machine.

As the Nineties lurched toward the new century, I grew more adept at my job. I slowly learned my way around the long, plastic hallway of thieves and pimps, while sharpening my instincts and figuring out the limitations of our space in the old mill. In those days, the touring industry's power brokers were the record labels and their complicit media, such as radio stations and print outlets, from *Rolling Stone* to the local entertainment rags. That powerful and mon-eyed infrastructure provided promoters cultural guideposts that simultaneously reflected and directed fans' tastes.

While print and broadcast media still traveled much faster than word-of-mouth did, they didn't have the lightning-viral velocity and reach of the soon-to-arrive Internet. Those same outlets were also far more concentrated and less fragmented than latter-day social networking. In other words, back in the analog days, a bazillion brands of cereal weren't spread all over a store the size of the Superdome, and the massive inventory didn't shift at the speed of sixty megabytes per second. Consequently, finding a few bands that folks wanted to see wasn't that particularly difficult.

At the same time, though, all that meant that "baby bands" had to work that much harder to make a name for themselves. Back then, an artist couldn't simply pop out a tune in fifteen minutes, slap it up on Myspace, Facebook or YouTube and send out a bunch of emails to create a fan base. The artists who rose out of their garages and onto the tiny stage at the old mill had to generate a buzz beyond, say, their parents. Once that buzz was loud enough for everyone to hear, including me, The Handlebar could exploit the band's nascent popularity. We could keep serving up everyone's favorite cereal.

And yet, I continued to insist on ignoring Livingston Taylor's number-one piece of advice. I continued to offer bloated guarantees for artists based on how much I loved their music. I frankly couldn't help myself from buying talent because of the talent, rather than whether or not anyone in town knew about a certain musician or cared enough to see him. Again going back to the blues: I consistently made bad deals on those shows because I refused to tune out what I thought was a buzz about the genre—a buzz, as it turned out, that existed mostly in my own head—but more than that I was addicted to booking legends. Give me Koko Taylor, James Cotton, Junior Wells and Jorma Kaukonen of Jefferson Airplane anytime. Never mind that too few people came to those shows.

During our years at the mill, a lot of regional bands did well, not just for themselves, but for us, too. These were the bands that had no record-label deals, but recorded, printed and sold their own CDs, thus paving the way for today's myriad indie labels that now rule the world. More than a few of these bands made a decent living just by playing the same clubs within driving range, often three or four times a year. We always counted on the likes of Uncle Mingo, with their pogo-stick antics and funk punk; Jump, Little Children, whose pop-rock drew hundreds of youngsters; Spartanburg's rockin' Albert Hill-renamed-Dezeray's Hammer; the Blue Dogs and their pre-Hootie frat-rock; Jupiter Coyote's pre-Phish jams; and Gran Torino, the horn-driven funksters from Knoxville, Tennessee. Almost every time these guys played, their shows slammed to the walls.

Then came the Internet and Napster and the ubiquity of the iPod. Those innovations helped dismantle the record labels and rearranged all traditional media. And next thing you know, the whole music and concert business went *kablooey*.

Let's leave it to business-administration grad schools and the burgeoning music-business education programs to figure out the whens, hows and whys of the industry's irrevocable spasms. Suffice to say that, as far as I was concerned, the biggest shifts came when the people who had always made the smallest investments and had taken the least risks filled the prevailing power vacuum. Those people owned or worked for the fast-growing talent agencies that lived off of their artist rosters and sought ever-bigger guarantees from promoters, as well as higher and higher ticket prices from fans. In short order, I found myself after 2001 stuck between the hard place of agents who wanted more and more money and the rock of struggling musicians who just wanted a place to play.

Despite the rising stakes and increasingly off-kilter priorities, the nuts and bolts of negotiations and artist contracts didn't change all that much. I could still book local bands and give them a door deal; that is, we simply paid them a percentage of the night's ticket receipts. Agents for national touring acts, of course, loathed offers like those—no guaranteed upfront commission in straight-percentage deals. Besides, an artist's guarantee always rose with her marquee value. Too many times in the last decade, an agent has told me: "My guy doesn't get out of bed for less than five grand," regardless of the artist's actual financial worth in a particular market. The B-52s, for instance, apparently won't play for a guarantee lower than a hundred-and-fifty thousand dollars. I even heard once that Aerosmith wouldn't consider a show at the local arena without seeing at least a nine-hundred-thousand-dollar offer.

Plenty of risks seemed worthwhile, of course. Others, though, just didn't make any sense, especially at first glance. Maybe that had more to do with the fact that, by the turn of the century, my crystal ball was becoming fuzzy with the new paradigm of escalating price tags—especially the ones attached to insta-stars. One day, for instance, I took a call from the same agency that had sold us John Mayer. The agent at that time called about a preternaturally talented and beautiful jazz-soul singer. I had only begun to hear a little bit about her, but not enough to take the risk that he wanted me to take; he was seeking an offer from me in the mid-four digits. My immediate reaction: No way. And definitely not on a Monday night, especially during the summer, our slowest time of year. The risk seemed and, just as importantly, *felt* absurd. And that is how I blew my one shot at booking Norah Jones. (In retrospect, it's entirely likely that given her pre-Grammy profile at the time, especially in our small market, the show would have bombed, financially, anyway.)

Here, then, stands the only principle in the loosely unprincipled business: There's no such thing as a bad show, just a bad deal.

To state again the tragically obvious, I had made plenty of bad deals during our mill days, but in our new location I was getting even better at agreeing to offer almost exactly what agents quoted for their bands. I was especially good at paying too much for artists whose local marquee value would only make sense months and sometimes years *after* their first show with us. I can't count the number of bands I've booked that drew thirty people in their Handlebar debut, only to sell out two-thousand seaters three months later. And how many times have we heard fans suggest that "you should book the Rising Stars," who, oh yeah, played in our near-empty room just a few months before?

I'll never forget the time that my brother called to ask me about an artist who had just become his brand-new favorite. Stephen had long since left our company, taking a pass on moving with us to our new location. He had had more than his fill of the music business, from which he never earned a dime, and he had to focus entirely on his day job and provide for his family, including his daughter, who was then on her way to college. And let's not forget that, back at the mill, I had all but shoved him into the kitchen and pushed him away from the sexiest role in the company—buying talent. (Even though he had the good sense to get out of the club business when he could, I still feel guilty about how *our* dream failed him.) At any rate, he asked me one day if I could snare him a couple of complimentary tickets to see his favorite new band at nearby Clemson University's Littlejohn Coliseum.

"Shouldn't be a problem," I said. "My smart and beautiful friend, Marty Kern, books the bands there, so I'll call and ask if she could spare a couple of house comps. Who did you want to see?"

"Zac Brown Band."

"Bite me."

"Huh?" He laughed. It was always pretty hard to hurt my brother's feelings because he was always too much of a good sport about …everything.

"Dude, Zac Brown has played our room *SIX TIMES*! It's not as if you would ever have to *buy a ticket* here. I mean, hell, you could've seen this guy to your heart's content, up close and personal."

"Uh, well, yeah, but I didn't know about him then."

"Oh, for god's sake, bro, it's not like I keep our artists a secret!"

Those darned Grammy Awards give away our artists every time; Zac had just won his first golden-gramophone statuette. I got my brother two tickets.

So Zac was another one who turned out to be a good deal, the kind that helps make up for so many bad ones. I would wager to say that I have concocted so many bad deals over the years that if I had never lost any money on any show since the beginning, we would long since have paid off all of our still-massive debts. But as the joke goes in the industry, and the concert business has only one joke: If you want to make a million dollars in the music business, you better start with two million.

Still, despite what anyone else says, a bad deal always hurts, it's almost always personal; a club owner's hard-earned money from last night just walked out the door tonight. Whenever that happens to a promoter, agents are quick to remind him: "Hey, nobody held a gun to your head. *You* were the one who wanted the date." More than once, I have pictured myself as Cleavon Little playing Sheriff Bart in *Blazing Saddles*, a film as convoluted and ridiculous as the concert industry. Every time that I have put together a big-dollar offer, I pictured myself holding a financial firearm to my head: "Don't nobody here move, or the promoter gets it."

Whenever the gun goes off, as it does whenever a show, as they say, "goes south," nobody seems to care. In fact, in an industry where *Schadenfreude* proves that misery really *does* love company, a similar sentiment once came from the owner of Washington, D.C.'s storied 9:30 Club. Seth Hurwitz, one of the country's sharpest promoters, once told the online trade 'zine *CelebrityAccess*:

> "I remember the first time we lost a lot of money on a show. We lost on all of them in the beginning. But it was a moment of clarity that I realized that these people (agents) don't give a fuck about me or my welfare. I don't know any other business where one part of the food chain, an important part of the food chain, has such a complete disregard for the health and welfare of another important part of the food chain."

That's because, Seth, too few people in the industry give a fuck about *the music*—except perhaps for the artists who make it, the promoters who buy it and the fans who consume it. And *those* are the very people who populate the dark floor of the "cruel and shallow money trench." As Buzz Osborne, singer for the influential sludge-rockers, The Melvins, put it best: "I've never met a group of people that hate music more than rock 'n' roll professionals."

Through the years, my own experiences with too many agents have piled up in a bitterness bin that requires routine cleaning. Screaming, cajoling, manipulating and threatening "never to do business with you again"; changing rules that only agents seem to know but dismissing them at will; and "negotiations" laced with all-too-personal remarks and patronizing comments—these are not-uncommon features of agent-promoter interactions. More than one agent has railed against my "attitude." What does that even *mean*, especially in the context of a buyer-seller transaction? Imagine walking into a wine shop with a wide-open checkbook, ample time to browse and the freedom to choose any appellation you want, from any of dozens of similar wine shops. Now imagine that you're surveying everything from Boone's Farm to a 1996 Chateau Haut-Brion, and the clerk says, "I don't like your attitude," when you tell him that you're declining to buy some bottle he's pitching at *his* price. And all of this nonsense, none of which belongs in any negotiation in the first place, pervades an industry that prides itself on relationships.

Here's just one example: We were about to lose substantial money on an artist who had done great business with us before. This time, though, ticket sales were shockingly lackluster. So in a panic that was meant to elicit some kind of compassionate response that might give Kathy and me a little relief, I called the agent to tell him about our stress.

"I don't need your fucking melodrama," he yelled. "Maybe you should look for another fucking line of work! It's a risk-based business."

No biggie. His artist won't play here again. And that's too bad, though not so much for the artist, whose agent will always find another venue, or for the fans, who will always find another favorite artist, but for the promoter who's only trying to serve both.

A Realtor friend once confided to me a story about the time he and two other real-estate guys played golf with Greenville's own homegrown music-success story, Edwin McCain. After a few rounds of back-slapping, high-fives, mutual admiration and good times, Edwin remarked to my friend something along the lines of, "Geez, Dan, if I'd been playing with a foursome from the music business, we would all be throwing our clubs at each other by now."

Still, a club promoter takes his best shot and just hopes to hit some green.

But yet, night after night, he finds himself at a crossroads where, like the legendary bluesman, he sells his soul for the sake of art and loses his mind in the process.

9

Anyone who loves art and who's still enough of a nihilist or narcissist to keep buying art for its quality, regardless of its financial return, should be rewarded, right? Every now and then, I was. One of the biggest and best rewards arrived in October 2003—just months before I suffered my first and worst major meltdown.

It was some time during the previous summer that I had gotten a call from Brian Swanson. I'd known Brian for years and liked working with him. He was one of those scarce, too-reasonable-for-the-business agents who at the time worked for Monterey Peninsula Artists. An industry heavyweight, Monterey represented the likes of Elton John, Dave Matthews Band and the Grateful Dead, and even some bands that we could afford. So Brian called to say that he was routing one of their artists. He wanted a particular date, but he warned me that he also sought a potentially bank-busting guarantee.

"The date we need is October Fifth," he said, "so we wanted to check your avails."

"Bummer," I said, "we're dark Sundays." Still, my curiosity compelled me to ask who he was pitching, in the unlikely event that we would agree to open and promote a show on the toughest day of the week.

"Would you be interested in Joan Baez?"

Would I be interested in Joan Baez? Would I be interested in winning the lottery so that I could book Bruce Springsteen? "Joan . . . Baez? Are you *serious?*"

"We're just checking."

Even before I consulted my internal and infernal Fan-O-Meter, I said, sure, we could see our way to opening on a Sunday.

Next, Brian and I talked numbers: ticket pricing, guarantee, the meat and bones of a potential offer. Within minutes, we struck a deal. I emailed him an offer, which Brian then forwarded to Joan's longtime manager. Once management approved the deal, Brian called back to confirm the show.

We announced almost immediately that Joan Baez would perform at The Handlebar!

Tickets sold out six weeks in advance.

The moment that Joan walked into our concert hall, I dissolved. I was struck by her grace and beauty, an ageless luminosity that belied her sixty-two years. I stood in the middle of the floor and told her that my brother, my wife and I had opened The Handlebar originally as a folk-music room, and that because she was the goddess of American folk music, why, she embodied everything that we had worked for.

"I just can't believe you're here," I said. My lower lip began trembling. "This means more to me than you can imagine."

I burst into tears.

She hugged me. I slobbered all over her shoulder, her white cotton blouse soaking up my sniffles. "That's the sweetest thing I ever heard," she said.

A few hours later, she put on one of the best shows in Handlebar history. She sprinkled her intimate and light-hearted stage presence with songs by Woody Guthrie and Ryan Adams and, of course, "The Night They Drove Ol' Dixie Down." During her set, she met the audience right at home.

"Did you hear the one about the two Southern belles sitting on the front porch?" she asked the packed house. In a surprisingly good Southern accent, she told the story of Sue Ellen boasting to Dorothy Belle about all the glittery gifts that her husband had bought for her.

"Sue Ellen said to Dorothy Belle, 'Do you see that Jaguar over there, that beautiful new car? My husband loves me so much, he up and bought that for me.' "

To which Dorothy Belle responded, "That's nice."

Then Sue Ellen showed her friend a sparkling ring. "It's a veritable rock. My husband loves me so much he buys anything I want."

To which Dorothy Belle again responded, "That's nice."

Perplexed about her friend's curt replies, Sue Ellen asked, "What'd your husband ever do for *you*?"

To which Dorothy Belle responded, "Well, he sent me to finishin' school."

"And why would he do anything like that?"

"Well, I used to say, 'Fuck you,' all the time, now I just say, 'That's nice.' "

Later, she sat on the edge of our stage and signed dozens of autographs and talked with fawning fans. All she asked of us, meanwhile, was that we turn down the air conditioner so that she could protect her throat. No hamsters, no tube socks, no all-white dressing room, just a high-wattage artist with low-energy needs.

But a club owner's not a real club owner unless he gets a lump or two from some customer or two at the end of just about every show. One ticket-buyer, for instance, stalked out after the concert to say he was disappointed: "I had no idea that she was so . . . *political*." Another patron said she would never return because we had over-charged her for her meal, by a dollar. We refunded her money, mostly because we had actually made some that night. (Still, those gripes didn't rise to the level of the single most unforgettable complaint. Before our Little Feat show, our kitchen had served a dinner special called "Dixie Chicken." Afterward, a customer demanded a refund and alleged "false advertising" because the band didn't play "Dixie Chicken.")

Despite the grievances, nothing will diminish the gift that Joan Baez gave to us—an enduring reminder about why we had gotten into this whole music thing in the first place.

And then just three months after that mountaintop experience, I plunged into an abyss.

On a cold Wednesday in early January 2004, we had Dirk Powell. Dirk was a nice guy and one of Nashville's finest studio musicians. Loretta Lynn and Jack White of the White Stripes and Grammy-winning producer T Bone Burnett all hired Dirk whenever they needed a world-class fiddler. The year before, Dirk had contributed to the soundtrack for *Cold Mountain*, based on Charles Frasier's blockbuster novel and starring Nicole Kidman, Jude Law and Renée Zellweger.

The film seemed destined for box-office success, and that was my expectation for our box office, too. I booked Dirk for a date just three weeks after the film's release. I had already convinced myself that the soundtrack would spark the same ticket-buying frenzy that we had seen with *O Brother, Where Art Thou?* After all, Dirk's name appeared in the list of credits, alongside the likes of Sting, Elvis Costello, Alison Krauss and the aforementioned Mr. White. Even Jude Law had been quoted as saying: "Hearing Dirk play the fiddle on the set of *Cold Mountain*, I felt as if my work as an actor had already been done for me."

But at The Handlebar on that frigid night in early 2004, something went terribly, horribly wrong.

For nearly twenty years leading up that moment, I had lived with grinding pain. The story's complicated. Suffice to say that my hips began to disintegrate soon after my kidney transplant in 1984, the result of a little-understood complication from the medications that I had to take to keep my body from rejecting my brother's alien body part. As the ball joints of my hips disintegrated, every step I took just meant that bone ground against bone. I walked with a conspicuous wobble and chronic agony.

In the years following the transplant, doctors told me to wait as long as I could, until I could no longer tolerate the pain, before they would agree to replace even one of my damaged hips. Their reasoning was that because I was young and active, I would wear out a titanium-and-plastic prosthesis quickly, thus creating direr complications. So I wobbled through the years, trying to suck up the pain and…failing miserably.

My uncle, Dr. John Feagin, a world-renowned orthopedic surgeon, had warned me at one time during these hellish years that while I couldn't run from the debilitating disease, literally, I couldn't hide from it, either.

"It's not the pain itself that makes you suffer," he said, "it's how the pain messes with your head."

So what to do? Writing helped. Promoting art helped a little, too.

As Kay Redfield Jamison explained in her compelling book, *Touched With Fire: Manic Depressive Illness and the Artistic Temperament*: "Creative work can act not only as a means of escape from pain, but also as a way of structuring chaotic emotions and thoughts, numbing pain through abstraction and the rigors of disciplined thought."

Meanwhile, my "creative work" had turned from transient newspaper reporter, always on the move, to talent buyer for a business that also required plenty of physical exertion.

Finally, in 1989, I couldn't take it anymore. I was living in Florida, where battalions of elderly folks were lining up for new hips. My uncle found a doctor who agreed to replace one of mine. But just one.

While that implant provided immediate relief on my left side, it didn't cut the pain in half. I still had a right long way to go. At the same time, the chronic pain continued wreaking havoc on my judgment. Judgment requires detachment. Pain undercuts objectivity, supplanting analytical thought with emotion. Emotion powers art—music. Operating in the business of music requires detachment. These jeopardized links in my internal chain could perhaps help explain a bit about how and why I often booked shows based on art and emotion, with imprudent or insufficient regard to business. Donald Trump's not a fan of real estate, he's a fan of money. One bad real estate deal costs money. In my case, people—musicians—were mobile real estate, to buy and resell. Sentiment, which art piques, has little to no room in business. Yet pain often fueled sentiment or, perhaps, the other way around, either way rendering me little more than a fan, a fan who wanted nothing more than to make the pain go away.

Pain trumped business.

Through the balance of fall 2003, we lost money on Steve Earle and Leon Russell. We lost money on a co-bill with The Waybacks and The Avett Brothers, the former going on to play arenas. (It has always struck me as yet another of the business's peculiar inequities that while an artist can go on to earn millions, one of his initial investors, that first small-club promoter, rarely if ever sees any return, although the buyer can boast, "We had John Mayer play here," or he might get a shout-out from the stratosphere.) We broke even on legendary trumpeter Maynard Ferguson and took a few hits on other shows, as well. By the end of that year, we saw attendance plummet fifteen percent from the year before. The drop was the result of a massive post-9/11 hangover, the official end of the Nineties' "irrational exuberance" and the beginning of a long, grinding economic slide. Add to all that the mounting chaos in the music industry's shifts to the Digital Age.

Autumn's string of losses—"bad deals"—contributed to escalating stress, which created an internal time bomb whose detonator ticked onward. I couldn't predict when the blast would blow me to bits.

Like everyone else, we crawled into 2004 with the usual high hopes for a fresh start. Most years began with a whimper; people are spent after the holidays, financially, spiritually and entertainmentally. In fact, only four days after New Year's, Sugarland returned, but fans didn't. Ticket sales for that Saturday night wound up forty percent lower than their first show in 2001, and gate receipts barely covered their guarantee.

Then came Dirk Powell.

I had booked the freshly minted *Cold Mountain* star for the Wednesday after Sugarland. Hump Day in the Bible Belt typically means Fellowship Night, so you might think that a show steeped in old-time Appalachian and gospel music might nudge God's marquee value at the local church just for one evening. You would think wrong. Still, I made what I thought was a reasonable offer for Dirk. The date routed well for him, his band and his agent, and routed shows generally mean lower guarantees. That's because agents can better distribute their artist's budgetary demands among the string of venues on the tour. Besides, *Cold Mountain* had outperformed the Coen Brothers flick at the box office, so how could we fail to see an *O, Brother* reprise?

O, brother…

The night began as they usually do, with the standard preparations and hopes for a crowd. Soon, though, my anxiety rose ever higher as I watched too few people trickle in. The minutes ticked by. My internal detonator ticked along with it.

As Dirk's show began winding down, I started working on settlement, counting the few bills from our ticket-desk cash register and filling out the Excel spreadsheet. We printed two copies of the Settlement Sheet, one that the tour manager signed for our recordkeeping and the other for him and his artist. I gazed at the finals:

Paid admissions: 48

Ticket price: $12

Gross gate: $576

Needless to say, ticket sales didn't come close to the guarantee.

What happened next, I still don't know.

I can only remember that I started wailing. Even now, I can picture myself tearing at my thinning, graying hair and howling in uncontrollable and incomprehensible despair.

Kathy moved up behind me and put her hands on my shoulders. Even now, I still can't imagine the confusion and fear that she must have been experiencing.

"How did this *happen*?" I cried. "What did I *do*, and what do we do *now*? How can we possibly pay this guy, where do we find the *money*?" I was thinking: Oh, my god, I have all of fifty-four dollars and change in my checking account! I can't even go to the ATM!

Her touch calmed me.

Soon, I quieted down and began rocking back and forth. At the same time, I somehow knew that I had turned white-sheet pale.

Then, oddly, I felt myself escape, hiding behind a protective wall of near-deliberate numbness. I had gotten pretty good at doing that. Over the course of eighteen surgeries since infancy, I had learned how to sail off, mentally, emotionally, spiritually and even in some physical way, to a safe, faraway place that was impervious to pain.

"It's okay," my wife said in her soft, velvety tone, which she enlists when the shit hits the fan. "We *have* the money, it's not that big a deal. It's just one show…"

I kept swaying, pasty and catatonic.

"Do you need to go to the doctor?" she asked. Her sweetness transcended judgment. Her kindness flowed with generosity—not with the sort of overbearing concern that often backfires on people who suffer. "We can go to the Emergency Room, we can call a doctor, go see someone…"

I was gone.

I don't even remember how I got home or what happened once I got there.

Only later did I realize that I must have experienced an honest-to-god nervous breakdown.

In the weeks that followed, Kathy asked that I stay away from the building. It wasn't safe for me there, she said, and I needed time and space to heal. As always, she was right. Still, she was forced yet again to carry the business alone. Fortunately, she could count on the all-encompassing help of our irreplaceable assistant, Meredith, who was capable of running the whole shootin' match if Kathy and I were to disappear.

I was the one, though, who did the disappearing. Having just been struck by who-knows-what, my mind the next day was as rattled as if I had fallen head first off some cliff and into some concussive dream-state. Any memories of those first few days and weeks either never existed or evaporated as quickly as new-fallen rain on a sun-shimmered street. I spent all that time resting and trying to recollect my wits, which apparently had just been blown to smithereens. While Kathy returned to even longer hours at The Handlebar, I mostly laid on our couch in something of a stupor that wore cotton drawstring "house trou," a T-shirt from some band and old dog-chewed slippers. That January, I barely ventured outside. Instead, I went inside, where my imagination had always provided the safest place for me during surgery or any other trauma.

Then one day, from out of nowhere, I started writing again. As the physical manifestation of a souped-up imagination, Art, with a capital A, always provided terrific—and cheap—therapy. So one day in the utter stillness of our house, I dreamed of a young accountant who had lost his job, but then decided that he had to find an old girl-friend, his last great love. So I started to write a novel. Once again, my own Art had pulled some semblance of sanity from the wreck-age of my incinerated nerves. And, yet, Kathy, who had given me the opportunity and resources to heal, continued to sacrifice herself for us and our business.

One night during my recuperation, Kathy suggested that I stop by The Handlebar for a bit, not long. She thought it might be good for me finally to get out of the house. Eddie From Ohio was playing a Friday night to a near-capacity crowd. What could be better, she told me, than to see a packed room and longtime friends? Their friendly foursome and their shows were always "safe," she said. I could be a fan again.

Since their first appearance way back in 1995, EFO always played for a shared-risk door deal, their hospitality and technical needs simple. They often brought creative initiatives, too. Once, they had hired a Grammy Award-winning producer to record a two-disc live album, *Portable EFO Show*, which included tracks from the mill and from The Barns of Wolf Trap in northern Virginia; I'm even on the record, introducing the band to a wildly enthusiastic crowd. Robbie, Mike, Eddie and Julie and their sound guy, Bob, had always been among the kindest artists in the business. They were practically family.

When I finally made my return to The Handlebar that bitter-cold night, I wore a parka and a ball cap pulled down to my eyebrows, to disguise my persistent puffiness. I dodged the crowd that filled the restaurant and went straight into the dressing room. The four were performing their pre-show ritual, huddling in something that resembled a small prayer meeting and a football team's hands-over-hands pep talk.

They made me feel at home again.

After that night, I tried as best I could to do the only things that I knew how to do. I booked bands, and I began to write again. The process provided precisely what Kay Redfield Jamison had written that it would: a creative means of escape. In three months, I completed the novel whose theme turned on reality vs. fantasy. I couldn't sell that manuscript, either, but that wasn't the point. The point was the process, as Kathy reminded me and Kay Jamison's book had told me, and the process was meant to help me dig out of my despair.

Meantime, Kathy fell into near-total ownership of the day-to-day operation, one that she had started with two brothers and their dream. Our partners contributed nothing, neither their own money—at least, none that wasn't fully repaid, with interest—nor their time, and I had spiraled into some degree of worthlessness. Hence, she found herself increasingly on her own to run the business. Gone now were the days when we could take a few nights off and enjoy each other's company. Her responsibilities and workload exploded, along with the hours she spent at work.

My wife had been raised in rural Missouri, just outside St. Louis, where hardworking people simply put one foot in front of the other and performed the job at hand. Only now her job had become a hydra whose multiple heads threatened to devour various or even all parts of her life, as well as our life together. Still, she wielded her Midwestern work ethic like a club, using her indomitable strength and unimpeachable integrity to battle the beast. To illustrate the spirit that she exudes: The Handlebar has seen precious little turnover; many of our employees have worked for Kathy for more than five years. That's a long stint in the service industry, where rampant personnel changes are the norm, but it's also testimony to the staff's loyalty to her and her leadership.

Despite her enormous accomplishments, Kathy has paid the price, financially, even physically and otherwise, at the very least wiping out her life savings that likely will never be repaid. Yet, she has purchased with all of that a corporate culture and a cohesive community that I believe will ultimately ensure a Herculean legacy for her. And while she continues battling away in her Second Labor against the many-headed beast of small-business management, she will always face remnants from her First Labor: taming me.

Things certainly didn't get any easier for her or for me when we again came face to face with yet another round of mission-distracting, anxiety-inducing and totally unnecessary bullshit.

In late spring 2004, just months after my crash, the State of South Carolina mailed us a notification: The Department of Revenue would send an auditor to examine all of our Admissions records for a three-year period, starting from March 2002.

We had always kept scrupulous records, all those tour-manager-signed Excel Settlement Sheets and every ticket stub from every show. Even before we opened for business, a state Revenue agent walked into the mill and told us that his office had seen press reports about a "new concert hall." Because we would be charging money for events, he said, we had to obtain an Amusement License, which meant that we would have to submit a monthly Admissions Tax return, along with a five-percent remittance on every ticket we sold. The state required us to store every bit of that stuff.

From the very first time I filed and paid our Admissions Tax, I bitched about it. The levy, I decided, couldn't possibly be fair. It seemed unlikely to me that the Revenue Department really collected money from *every single establishment* that sold tickets in the state, from movie theaters to hole-in-the-wall dives that charged a cover to backwoods biker bars with three-dollar bands. So I launched a crusade. I wrote and called everyone I could think of: our attorney, the inestimable Frank Eppes; our then-U.S. Senator, the wizened states-man Strom Thurmond; our U.S. Congressman; our state House rep-resentative; friends in the various media; and even DOR employees. All of them said their hands were tied. The law was the law, they all said, render under Caesar his Coliseum tax.

"There is just *no way* that this tax is uniformly enforced," I ranted once to a hapless Revenue clerk.

"That's probably true," she told me, "but the thing is, hon, our agents don't like to work on Friday and Saturday nights." Then, she added, in that down-home way that was supposed to make me feel better: "Look on the bright side, you pay *eighteen* different taxes."

Of course, yes, *riiight*! But even then her list didn't include the federal Bureau of Alcohol, Tobacco and Firearms' annual two-hun-dred-and-fifty-dollar alcohol stamp, which the Feds finally discontinued after realizing that the tariff was originally enacted to finance the Spanish-American War. And the state Revenue lady also didn't mention yet another levy, the City of Greenville's two-percent hospitality tax on all food and beverage, which, everyone knows, includes a whopping amount of alcohol. By ordinance, all those revenues are earmarked for "tourist infrastructure." Not long after the tax collections began, the City gave one-hundred and fifty-thousand dollars to Bob Jones University for its renowned museum and gallery, considered one of the finest Christian-art collections in the world and apparently a worthy tourist destination. Somehow, though, the fundamentalist-evangelical institution had no problem accepting alcohol-drenched tax revenues.

Okay, so, anyway: In its audit notification, the state of South Carolina told us to gather up all of our records for their specified three-year period—ticket stubs, artist contracts, the works.

A state employee named Rickey Pulley walked in a couple of months later. Mr. Pulley was a quiet, unassuming bureaucrat who assured us that he wouldn't be in our way, he was just doing his job.

I took him back to one of our dressing rooms, now filled with every shred of the requested documentation. I waved toward the twenty-two cardboard bankers' boxes jammed with manila envelopes that themselves were stuffed with cardstock ticket stubs. Each stub represented every fan who had bought a ticket for one of nearly three-hundred and fifty shows that the state wanted to audit.

Mr. Pulley stood motionless and speechless. His eyes grew the size of guitar picks. His jaw fell.

"This *is* everything y'all wanted, right?" I said, trying to keep the snark off my smile.

He nodded and chuckled one of those *oh-shit* chuckles.

For the next three months, he worked from nine or ten in the morning until about five at night. He stopped only for a lunch of Doritos and a soft drink. Hour after hour, day after day, month after summer month, he sat in that small, windowless room and counted

…every…single…ticket stub…from every single show…from every last one of those hundreds of manila envelopes. He never touched the foot-high stack of artist contracts.

In August, he finally emerged with his report. He found that our accounting had been off by about three-thousand tickets. Because we had sold nearly *sixty-seven thousand* of them during the audit period, we considered that our error rate of about a half of one percent wasn't too shabby.

The DOR subsequently billed us twenty-six hundred dollars in "penalties and interest" for those discrepancies. At the same time, we could never muster the courage to ask the state how much the Revenue Department had spent on Mr. Pulley's summertime residency in our dressing room.

A few months later, I was jolted awake at about 4 in the morning. Red-hot pain exploded from my right hip.

Remember that my decayed left hip had been replaced in 1989, but the prosthesis failed, a common problem, especially among active youngsters and especially after a decade of heavy use. That replacement then got replaced in 1999, in the summer before The Handlebar was thrown out of the mill.

Now, though, in early autumn 2004, my still-untreated right hip finally collapsed. The ball that fit into the pelvic socket would look on an X-ray like a crushed Ping Pong ball. My leg shortened about a quarter of an inch.

The agony shot through me.

My groaning woke up my wife, who immediately called the doctor. Minutes later, she raced to the twenty-four-hour drugstore to fill a prescription of fabulous narcotics. She stayed awake until I passed out. As soon as the orthopedist's office opened several hours later, we went in to schedule another hip-replacement surgery. Which meant that I would spend yet *another* six weeks off my feet, recuperating away from The Handlebar, though I could still work the phones and my laptop from the bed, first at the hospital, then at home. It also meant that I was again abandoning Kathy to run the business by herself, a role that she more or less had already taken and would ultimately take for good.

The surgery proved to be relatively easy and a huge success, rendering me absolutely pain-free after eighteen years of wobbling around in chronic agony, pain that had helped destroy my newspaper career and had helped propel me to seek some strange redemption in an impossible dream.

And so after finally getting back on my feet again, this time literally, I didn't have to wait long for yet another kick in the ass.

In early 2005, our company was served with a forty-thousand-dollar lawsuit.

A little background: If you've ever happened to look at a song title on the back of a CD booklet or album sleeve, you may have noticed some small type next to the artist's name: BMI, ASCAP or SESAC. The acronyms stand for Broadcast Music Inc. (BMI); the American Society of Composers, Authors and Publishers (ASCAP); and the Society of European Stage Authors & Composers (SESAC—yes, *European*). These three supposedly nonprofit Performing-Rights Organizations, or PROs, were formed in the last century to insure that artists receive their due royalties. Congress has since given the PROs a legal mandate to protect copyrights for the millions of songs in their respective "repertoires"—essentially, *any* song that's performed *anywhere* in public: live events and broadcasts, even recorded music that's played on a meat-market jukebox. Every business that airs music to anyone who might hear it, from a karaoke bar to a pizza parlor, is required to purchase a license from all three PROs. (So, yes, these are the very rules and enforcement organizations that we have to thank for giving the world Muzak, which was founded to pay all those licensing/copyright fees for all that delightful elevator music.)

The trouble is that these licenses are—you guessed it—expensive: thousands of dollars a year, payable to the PROs.

These businesses price their blanket permits according to esoteric formulas that are generally based on a venue's capacity; frequency of performance(s); and a few other factors. The PROs argue that a license allows the licensee to play all the copyrighted music he wants to play because, now, he doesn't have to keep track of every song in those three vast repertoires, which everyone knows would be impossible, anyway. In a sense, then, the PROs consider their legally mandated licenses as insurance, of sorts—*just in case* you played a copyrighted song. The biggest licensees, of course, are radio and TV broadcasters, arenas, festivals and the like. And from those billions of dollars in fees, the PROs ostensibly distribute royalties to their hundreds of thousands of member artists, all of whom have registered their works with at least one of them. Obviously, all three claim that their royalty payments are fairly distributed.

But…

Let's say that we pay a performer five thousand dollars for a seventy-five minute show. Let's say that she sings all of her own material, except for three cover tunes. And let's say that we lose our ass on her guarantee. Just like the state Admissions Tax, we *still* owe the licensing fees because, hey, the writers of those three covers are entitled to royalties—entitled, that is, to some of the money that those, let's say, fifty people paid for the show, whether they even wanted to hear, let alone *did* hear, those particular songs or not. At the same time, the performer supposedly also receives royalties for playing her *own* music, even though we had already paid her plenty enough.

Complex and dry as all that may be, the bottom line is that the fan gets screwed yet again: those costs, like well-dressed hamsters and bitchy tour managers, are built into the price of every ticket. And does all that money really go to the artists who have actually earned it?

The whole arrangement never did make any sense to me. I got

even more miffed about the entire racket when I finally got my first novel published. It seemed to me that because my book sat on library shelves everywhere and readers passed copies amongst themselves and that people sold their used hardbacks online—why, shouldn't I be entitled to royalties from all those readers who hadn't paid for the original copy? Where are the PROs for writers whose works float around the same way that songs do? I mean, I wasn't making any money off my "used" book. Why should artists make money off their "used" songs?

On top of being confounding, intrusive and occasionally frightening, the unruly and unfair system often gets silly.

In 1995, ASCAP sued the Girl Scouts. The PRO sought damages from campers for singing campfire songs that included "Puff the Magic Dragon" and "God Bless America." Evidently, the camps where these criminal copyright infringements had occurred had failed to obtain licenses. Either the camp directors had never realized that they were stealing someone's music, or they simply couldn't afford the outrageous fees. Thanks to the subsequent public-relations firestorm that blistered ASCAP, the suit went away.

But that hasn't stopped the PROs from filing thousands of these lawsuits every year, against damn near everyone.

To initiate their legal action against us, BMI dispatched spies to The Handlebar.

On three separate occasions, BMI's agents, who entered our building incognito, noted that they heard compositions from BMI's sprawling repertoire: "Last Train to Georgia"; "Workin' Man Blues," an appropriate tune; and "Rocky Top," which, incidentally, is owned by the founders of—wait for it—BMI. You've got to wonder just how big a fortune that single song has earned those people.

In any event, company lawyers later alleged that because we didn't have a license at the time to play those BMI songs in public, we owed their artists *forty-thousand dollars* in damages. For three songs. A few bars that happened to be performed in front of a whole lot fewer people than the full-capacity attendance figures on which BMI's suit was based.

As soon as we got served with the suit, I called Frank, our unflappable, indispensible lawyer. Next, I called a friend at *TIME* magazine, a former colleague from back in my newspaper days. In a jiffy, one of *TIME's* stringers showed up to interview me about the crushing litigation, as well as the possibility that Congress might revisit the heinous Copyright Act of 1976, which was partly responsible for all of this. Finally, I called our then-Congressman, Bob Inglis, a Greenville Republican who himself had been threatened for using a song snippet during one of his campaign events.

In short order, Inglis and his aide, Wayne Roper, appeared at The Handlebar and listened to me seethe before they had to return to D.C. A day or so later, they dialed up a conference call that also included three BMI bigwigs, Frank and me.

Thus commenced a remarkable smackdown.

"I don't know who you people think you are," Mr. Inglis said in his firm-but-diplomatic Congressional tone, "but not too long ago, another one of my constituents, a young man who runs a pizza joint, told me that you sent one of your spies—"

"They aren't spies," one of the BMI-voices said.

"Let me finish, please. I was saying that you sent one of your spies into his pizza restaurant and, even though nobody was in the place at the time, there was music playing, and your guy started going after the employee."

Yeah, Congressman, go get 'em! Take that, you big-money, fancy-suit goons!

Then, even though I could almost see Frank wincing with my every word, I unloaded: "Excuse me, Congressman, but let me get this straight. You BMI thugs can just walk into any privately owned company any time you want to, without any announcement—or invitation—and then go around suing anybody you want to and shake them down for exorbitant and essentially arbitrary fees that you say you distribute to . . . who, exactly?"

"We pay eighty percent of our revenues to our member songwriters," another BMI-voice said.

"Is that so?" (I somehow restrained myself from adding: "That is such horseshit.") But I *did* say, "Lemme tell you something. I know several BMI members"—I named a few local musicians—"and all of them have had their songs played on the radio *somewhere*, and they have all performed here. And you know how much they get in royalties from you people?" (I managed to keep myself from yelling: "They don't get diddly-squat!") "You know how I know that? It's right there on your Website! You say that most of the billions that you rake in from your Congressionally authorized swindle goes to those artists who rack up the highest touring revenues. That's right, the bulk of the cheese goes to artists like the Rolling Stones, U2, Dave Matthews Band and . . . no, *not* your little-known local songwriters!" Something along those lines, if perhaps in a more civil, if still simmering, tone.

After awhile, Inglis and I had our fill of slapping BMI around. They hung up. I stayed on the phone with my democratically elected representative.

"You would've made a pretty good lawyer," he said.

The suit was settled out of court, for some kind of judgment against me personally and demands that we pay BMI money that we wouldn't have for a scheme that just didn't make much sense.

Often lost amid the madding machinery of PROs, taxes, general-liability and workers-comp and liquor-liability and health insurance bills, city, state and federal bureaucracies and ordinances, utility bills, vendors, staff, fans and all the rest—somewhere in all of that commercial chaos are the artists. Despite *my* occasional bad deal, *they* almost always put on a good show. That's their job. Some are pretty damned good at it. But only the rare ones know much about business, and yet it's the artists who define the very *raison d'être* of our entire industry. They're the sole and entire reason that some agents make mountains of money and the rest of us sell buckets of beer.

Some musicians are your basic scruffy kids who simply want to live the rock 'n' roll lifestyle. Some are angst-ridden social misfits who happen to write great songs. Most seem as if talent or circumstance has forced them to do what their Creator wired them to do. Some of them are divas, some are douche-bags and some are delusional. More often than not, though, they are *nice people* who also happen to be thankful for a place to play, a hot meal and, if possible, a shower. They also get to see the world, while earning, some of them, a pretty good living. And as much as it's become a cliché, they're also addicted to whatever goes on in the dressing rooms and tour buses, along with the applause they crave.

When artists who don't handle business all that well try to handle business, things can go haywire quickly, and when they involve their family members, things can get even worse.

To illustrate: One night, a performer, who is widely considered one of the country's top acoustic musicians, sent his wife into our office to settle the show. Most of the time, promoters deal with a professional tour manager, who gets paid to handle the filthy lucre. The TM then thanks the venue owner for his band's pay and the hospitality, has a drink or two, returns to the bus and leaves. Of course, we all know that settlement can turn into a nightmare when the TM happens to be a Denise or a Thunderbirds Brian. Rarely, and especially with national touring bands, do you deal with an artist or his spouse. But on the night in question, things went from weird to tragic.

We had offered the acoustic giant a substantial guarantee. The deal also was structured in a way that's common throughout the industry: if the show sold X number of tickets, then the artist would "go into points," as they say, earning a bonus on top of his guarantee.

As the concert hall emptied, we printed our standard Settlement Sheet. The finals, as they're called, showed that three-hundred and ninety-six people bought a ticket, and the sheet reflected an *additional* twenty-odd people who had been put on the artists' guest list. That's an obnoxiously high number because the promoter doesn't earn any money from complimentary tickets, but in this case, obviously, the artist had a lot of friends in town. In any event, the numbers showed the artist going into points, so we had to add several hundred dollars to his already-decent guarantee.

The artist's wife looked at the sheet and began shaking her head. "No way."

"No way…what?" I wasn't just nonplussed, I was flabbergasted, on the way to getting pissed off.

"There were more than four hundred people in the room."

"Yes, in fact, there were. Three-hundred and ninety-six plus twenty-three comps equals four-nineteen. Which, in fact, is more than four-hundred people."

"But there were more than four-hundred *paid*."

Actually, no, in fact, there weren't. No matter how hard or how long or how much I tried to explain, she wasn't buying. I offered to show her all the ticket stubs, as we had done for the state auditor. I offered to show her the stack of tickets that we had printed but hadn't sold, known as "deadwood," hard evidence for unsold tickets. I offered to let her go in and count the chairs that we had put down, which numbered about three-hundred and fifty; several fans had preferred to stand.

After *waaaay* too much drama, she finally accepted the settlement, and they left.

A few weeks later, though, our intern, Charlie, ran into them at another event.

"I just saw you at the place where I work, The Handlebar," he said.

"Yeah," the artist said, "I was just there. And that place ripped me off."

When Charlie told me that, I immediately picked up the phone and called the agent. "You tell that sonofabitch, first of all, that he questioned the very integrity on which everything I do in this business is built and he said so to a complete stranger, and, second, if he says one more thing—just one—that defames me or my company in public, you'll get a letter from our attorney. *Capice*?"

In an industry whose existence relies on a principle so delicate as trust, we couldn't afford for anyone—the IRS, the state, our partners, banks and creditors, agents and artists, no one—to consider even the slightest doubt about the irreproachable way we ran our business.

At the end of the day, and night, the simplicity of common integrity helps explain why we've been around all this time. That—along with a handful of artists who have saved us tons of money because they believed in what we were trying to do as much as we believed in them.

Case in point: Dar Williams one night bowled Kathy and me over with her compassionate generosity. I had long been a fan of the mystically talented songwriter/poet whose endearing smile and arresting intelligence have made her a rare breed in the business. Naturally, my Inner Fan had reared its perilous head when I made the deal.

At show's end, the numbers looked dismal. When Dar began talking to us about settlement, we tried to conceal the stress that had been building up in us for weeks. Standing by one of the server stations, she casually asked about the finals.

We swallowed hard and told her.

She thought for a second about the situation, then said, "Y'know, it's funny. When I looked at my itinerary and saw your offer to my agent, it sort of stood out. I thought, 'Gee, that seems high, even out of line with the rest of the guarantees on my tour.' "

Kathy and I just stood there, watching and waiting and listening.

"I'll tell you what, guys, how about if I take $_____, rather than the whole amount that's on the contract?" She named the sum total of the night's gate receipts.

With immense relief and gushing gratitude, we hugged her and praised her willingness to help us and our company.

"Geez," she said with a sympathetic smile, "no *wonder* you two have been so stressed out all this time!"

All that might come off as "fucking melodrama," but guess what? Dar Williams can play our room any time she wants to.

And while all the various anxieties continued, the stars occasionally did drop in from out of nowhere. It was around the time of our legal collision with BMI that one of them pulled up to our place to play.

That spring evening, while enthralled fans gathered in the concert hall, I stood out in our load-in area on a breathtaking twilight. There, I chit-chatted with none other than John Hiatt.

"We just had Joan Baez here," I told him with no small pride. "She was incredible. I mean, I slobbered all over her shoulder." He shot me a nervous glance. "No worries, man. I'm a huge fan of yours, of course, but I won't slobber all over your shoulder."

"Y'know," he laughed, "if she were here right now, I think I'd probably slobber all over her shoulder, too."

He put on one hell of a show. Just him and his guitar. He sang his hits, songs that everyone knew. He told a ten-minute tale about a twenty-year argument that he'd had with his wife about which way the toilet paper goes in the holder. And he'd been as down-to-earth and easygoing as his hospitality rider: just a few beverages and a fresh-roasted chicken—how many dried-out, curled-up deli-meat slices should a genuine rock 'n' roll hero have to endure?

If only the business of the music business always operated the way it did that one unforgettable night. In that sense, buying talent for a small club is sort of like playing golf. When you hit that soaring drive, or you drop that sixteen-foot putt, or you score an eagle on that one nettlesome hole—those are the times that make all those slices, sandpits and shots into the woods go away. You can't wait to return to the course and take another swing.

Coda

At the end of the story, wherever that may lead and whatever that may be, we all of us just want to leave behind a worthwhile and lasting legacy. Some leave children, some money, some art, and a few of the more fortunate among us bequeath all or many of those. For lots of people, it seems, simply leaving behind an enduring string of cherished memories make a pretty good bequest.

If that's a respectable goal in life, I guess I could persuade myself into believing that, despite the setbacks, obstacles, frustrations, disappointments and such, I have helped share and have experienced for myself, too, enough memories to last a few lifetimes.

Mission accomplished—maybe.

Perhaps anything that The Handlebar achieved has come only by dint of sheer longevity or just a critical mass of fans. After promoting nearly three-thousand artists who have played for more than a quarter of a million ticket-buyers—and counting—it seems likely that The Handlebar has touched and maybe still might touch at least one of them.

The small listening room in Greenville, South Carolina, now

attracts a second generation of fans, perhaps even the grandchildren of those live-music supporters and aficionados who took the first intrepid steps into the dark, creepy halls of the mill. Every now and then, a customer whose parents had first brought him to a show will appear at The Handlebar. One day, Kathy saw a kid who dropped in from the past. The young man was as tall as a crape myrtle with hair just as big around. Of course, she recognized him, one of Tom and Meg's two boys. Their parents started bringing them to shows for as long as anyone can remember. These kids weren't boys anymore. Old enough to drink now, he ordered a beer and picked up a couple of tickets for another show.

We even heard that Evan Dehner had returned to South Carolina. Remember him—that enormously gifted kid who had opened for Keb' Mo' and joined him on stage in one of the best encores ever? He's welcome back any time he wants to play.

So we may not have made much in the way of money, but we've made some friends, and we've made a community. In our world, we've seen births and deaths and weddings, the whole cradle-to-grave cycle that makes the stuff of songs, of art, of life in its entirety. We even played host to a party once for a couple that wanted to have their "Harley wedding" at The Handlebar. They rented the venue and parked his-and-her Hawgs on either side of a makeshift altar in front of the stage. The bride wore white chaps. After the ceremony, the newlyweds rode over the concrete floor, through the double doors of the concert hall and out into forever. Another time, folks held a wake for a friend and regular who had died too soon. His last requests included a big party with barbecue, a band and everyone wearing Hawaiian shirts. Then someone sprinkled a loved one's ashes on the dance floor while Tower of Power played because the departed's friends wanted to dance with him one last time, along with his favorite band. Now we're just waiting for anybody who wants a baptism.

The circle of life goes on. The music always plays.

Still, The Handlebar likely won't be around forever. Few small venues last a lifetime. The Cavern Club, the former bomb shelter where the Beatles played nearly three hundred shows before they became the biggest band in history, has long since closed. London's Marquee club, where the Who got started, is shuttered. Gerdes Folk City, the West Village club where Dylan played his first professional gig, passed into history, though it did hang on longer than most—nearly forty years. The Stone Pony, where Springsteen rocked Asbury Park, New Jersey, closed and opened a few times in the 1990s, reopened in 2000 and operates anew. Oh, and club Luna in Santa Fe, where Kathy and I had seen Tish Hinojosa during our honeymoon trip so many years before? We heard that shortly after the Smashing Pumpkins played there, the place died.

The continuity of live music speaks more to the tenacity of the art and the fans who keep it going—not so much to the transitory buyers and brokers who wedge themselves between the performer and the patron. In a perfect world, Commerce gets out of the way of Art that then has the room to do what it's supposed to do: entertain, educate and inspire. Those of us on the business side of things just need to do a much better job of getting out of the way.

The thing is, though, that the cruel and shallow trench shouldn't have to be a grave.

Mike's a big, affable, lovable guy who loves heavy metal and loves The Handlebar. He's one of our bartenders and has been for years, since we plucked him from the remnants of Occasionally Blues. One day, he asked me about this Handlebar book that I was writing.

"Does anybody die at the end?"

"Oh, yeah," I told him, "Of course someone dies, dude, we've been here for nearly eighteen years. Y'know, like, Herb."

Not *that* Herb, not our friend who warned us about getting into bed with complete strangers, partners about whom we knew absolutely nothing. No, *that* Herb is as different from the other Herb as punk rock is from folk music. *This* Herb—we'll call him Herb—was an iconoclast if there ever was one.

Not long after we opened, Herb showed up at our doorstep like some stray mongrel who only wanted attention, love and family, and more than that: music. Herb loved music as much as a dog loves to chase cats and bark at things that aren't there. He was a skinny, scrawny guy, an older gent who tended toward the dapper. He often sported suspenders and a tam and a tweed coat.

"I'm a lighting guy," he announced when he walked in that day. "I run stage lights and have for years. I've run lights for just about anybody you can think of. I used to tour with the Fabulous Thunderbirds."

Oh, swell. Did you ever know a guy named Brian? It turned out that he had never met the cranky Briton. Herb had ridden the T-birds' bus long before any Brian jumped on board.

All that's pretty cool, we told him, but we don't have any money to hire a lighting tech.

"I'll work for free."

We now had a light guy…and a man with enough stories to fill a book twice the length of this one.

Herb was a veteran of the United States Army and had served just a few years, including, if I'm not mistaken, a stint in Vietnam. He was once stationed in Europe, too, where he told us about the three years that he had spent in a Spanish prison. Seems he had gotten busted while running a load of dope from Morocco or some-damn-place en route to the Netherlands and wound up behind bars.

The timeline's a little fuzzy, mostly because Herb was. The man simply had so many stories that they didn't so much as blur together as they all collided, like one huge train wreck on the zig-zaggiest track of life that you can imagine.

He had also done what real hardcore stoners did in the early '70s—he traveled the Hippie Trail, the wildly exotic trip that started in London or Amsterdam and wound through Turkey and the Middle East, on to Afghanistan, then India and ultimately, for some, to Australia. Herb got only as far as Kabul, where he partook in monster quantities of opiates and god-only-knows-what else.

Ultimately, he wound up in Austin, where he fell in with the T-Birds, as well as some of the clubs around town.

"Did I ever tell you about the time," he said, "when Janis Joplin used to babysit me and my brother?"

Yes, Herb, you did, a whole bunch of times.

When I booked Commander Cody or Johnny Winter or, really, pretty much anybody from Back In The Day, it always happened that some grizzled old roadie or sound guy or bus driver would get off the bus, take one look at Herb and say:

"Well, I'll be damned, if it ain't ol' Herb Royé." Followed by big hugs that could break the poor guy into multiple, worn-out pieces. "Man, last time I saw you was in Austin, where you were running lights with . . . " And, sure enough, it would be anybody from Janis Joplin to just about everyone else Herb had ever named.

One of Johnny Winter's hirsute guys stepped off the RV and took one look at Herb: "Holy shit, it's Herb! I haven't seen you since the old Armadillo days."

The Armadillo World Headquarters was one of Herb's most cherished stops along his way. The storied Austin, Texas, nightclub had been the center of Herb's universe for years, and damned if he doesn't appear in a 1976 newspaper clipping from an old counterculture weekly, the Austin *Sun*:

"Armadillo personnel additions include new stage manager Herb Royé, a veteran of Woodstock and the Monterrey [*sic*] Pop festivals and the Rolling Stones."

Okay, well. Sure, Woodstock may have included a half-a-million people, but what were the chances that more than one Herb Royé was among them?

When Joan Baez got off her bus, she took one look at Herb and said. "Oh, my gosh. I remember you from Woodstock. You were the guy on the white horse!"

As for the *Sun's* mention of Herb's stint with the Stones, well, he never did mention that, but Ms. Baez pretty much sewed up Herb's credibility.

More than all of his wacky stories and adventures, Herb loved music, and he loved lights and the gels that he lovingly changed out on the par cans that washed our stage with reds and blues and ambers. He was an *artiste*. He took his work as seriously as anybody who ever played an instrument under his lighting designs. He preferred crimsons and total darkness. He manipulated the lights along with the mood of the songs, though his colors didn't always gibe with the sounds onstage.

"What the hell's going on?" one band member said over the crowd when Herb had gotten especially frisky on his lighting console. He had been running the faders like some blues shredder ripping up and down a fret board. "Does the light guy back there think this is this some fucking disco?"

Another time, Los Straitjackets, a surf-rock band known for the Mexican wrestling masks they wore during their shows, lobbed another grenade at Herb across the room.

"Dude," one of them said, "we're all wearing masks up here, and it's hard enough to see without the lights going out every now and then."

Because Herb was an artist, he took any and every gripe personally, especially the ones that hit him across a room full of people. Clearly hurt, he would take his hands off the lighting board, lean back on his stool in the sound booth and proceed to sulk for the rest of the night.

Poor Herb.

And he *was* poor, too. From time to time, he skulked to the office and begged Kathy or me for twenty dollars to get him through the next day or so. We always fed him, but he needed money for booze and cigarettes and whatever else would kill him.

"That shit'll kill you one day," I told him more than a few times. I

teased him mercilessly, but he had done it all, seen it all, heard it all—
the stuff that makes a good sport of just about anybody.

At the beginning of nearly every show, I always told him: "Don't
forget the house lights, Herb." Sometimes I had to remind him of that
even after the band had taken the stage, despite the fact that leaving
the house lights on didn't show off his artistic flair. We once gave him
a T-shirt that said: "Don't forget the house lights, Herb." He used to
wear it under his tweed jacket and suspenders.

As I began stepping up our hard-rock offerings, several industri-
al-strength bands required that we erect a barricade in front of the
stage. Barricades are standard hardware at arena shows, barring fans
from the proscenium and protecting the band from concertgoers
who become particularly wound up during high-octane shows.

Herb sneered at me when he saw the first one go up. "Nothing
says Handlebar like a barricade."

"Fuck you, Herb. If this is the only way we can make any money
so that we can bring in those Texas guys you like so much, well, that's
just the way it has to be."

As time crawled on for Herb, he kept taking turns for the worse,
but he always showed up to run lights. More and more, he traveled to
get some kind of treatment or another at the VA Hospital in Columbia, about an hour-and-a-half away. I'm not sure that Herb even
owned a car. He always walked to The Handlebar from the ramshack-
le, two-story house that he shared with his brother a couple of miles
away. One time, the Army decided that it owed him some money for
some reason. He received a windfall of several thousands of dollars,
which he promptly blew on god-knows-what, probably everything
from more booze and more cigarettes to more coke. Apparently, he
shared lavishly, if not with the cash, at least with his stash.

Then one day, our longtime friend and Handlebar devotee, Lynn
Cusick, stopped in. She worked for Hospice.

That was around the time that Sean LaRoche died, but I still
somehow believed that hospice was just another name for a nursing

home, a place where old people went when they were in particularly bad shape. I just didn't *want* to understand that hospice meant the end of the line.

"That crazy bastard!" I said. "Here he goes again. I mean, hell, the guy's been on death's door so many times that the Grim Reaper probably thinks Herb's just up to his usual hijinks, putting a bag of cow shit on the front porch and lighting it up."

Lynn looked a little hurt, mystified and probably a bit angry at my unseemly, insensitive outburst. I simply couldn't and wouldn't admit that good ol' Herb wouldn't be around with his wild stories, goofy smile and abiding passion for the music.

The next day, Kathy and I went by to see him. The afternoon was cold and gray. His house was jammed with books, the walls lined with posters from old rock shows, more than a few that he had taken from The Handlebar and had gotten signed by his favorite artists.

He was laid out in his king-sized bed in his darkened, cluttered room. He looked even worse than usual, tragically thin, wasting away from cancer and every-damn-thing else. But the light was still with him. God was still at the console, making sure the faders were still bright enough in him. He sounded feeble, but he sounded hopeful, too.

"Who do you have coming up that you need me to run lights for?"

"Herb," I said, "you're pissing me off. My first novel's about to come out, and if you don't read it, I'll have to kick your ass."

He laughed and told me not to worry about it, he couldn't wait to get it.

Kathy, meanwhile, was her usual gentle loving self. She told Herb that she hoped he would come back soon. She knew that he never would.

He died the next day.

Herb's memory lives on, like one of those classic-rock songs that you just can't get out of your head, the melody and lyrics triggering memories, some that make you laugh, some that make you cry, some that take you back to the best times of your life.

Herb lives on as an example to every one of us in this insane business, from the artist to the agent, from the promoter to the manager, from the bartender to the fan. We're all in this for one reason: to see the world in a different light through the lens of sound, of stories told to song, to hear the human condition from those who have the gifts and guts to sing it in ways that most of us mere mortals simply can't.

Here, then, the final notes: Regardless of what happens to The Handlebar and to those of us who put our lives into it, whether our business lives longer than we do or passes too soon the way Herb did, I suppose I can tell myself that I did the best I could.

In these past couple of years, I haven't spent much time at the venue that my brother and I had dreamed so long ago to open. I can do much of my work—buying talent—on my laptop and cell phone, joining so many others in this business of music who have gotten away from the live experience and turn their focus instead on survival.

Despite that, I am still a fan and always will be, reveling in the very melodrama that's often required to create good art. If that costs us a fortune, so be it. Still, I hope that this business doesn't cost much more than money, that it doesn't liquidate what's left of health, happiness and sanity—primarily Kathy's, because, anymore, thanks to my acknowledged limitations, she's the one who puts in grueling hours to run a dream that wasn't originally hers. And I hope that we will somehow be able to celebrate the myriad unforgettable moments, the way we did when we held each other during our final moments together at the old mill. And, finally, whenever all may be said, sung, played and done, I hope that my baby brother might look back at this half-cocked, cockamamie idea and say, "Dude, you used my gift pretty well."

Liner Notes

When a band's up on stage, you think: Wow, those four guys got it goin' on! The reality is that a startling array of people helped put them there—and that's not even counting all their adoring fans. The same thing's true for this book and the monumental, life-filling enterprise behind it.

First and foremost, my heart and thanks, love and admiration, respect and awe go to my wife and business partner, Kathy Laughlin. I would be nothing without her, and without her, the world would have no Handlebar and no story about it, either.

As for the nearly quarter-million ticket-buyers who have given my wife and me a living and all of the bands and artists who have brought us those patrons and fans, it's perforce impossible to name them all. Still, I thank them, especially those who believed in us and our mission and have helped us survive.

Through all these years, hundreds of people, perhaps even thousands, have supported us, pitching in and giving their time, talents, money, effort, love and so much more.

In making this list, I know that I will leave out too many people, and for that I am sorry. Still, I want to name a few, and, in no particular order, with my deep and abiding appreciation: Frank Eppes, Gene Berger, Tommy Brown, Page Priest, Kelly and Freddie Wooten, Bo Terry, Tripp Yeargin, Julia Price, Ed Martz, Willis Tisdale, Will McKibbon, Steve Shrum, Lisa and Max Shanks, Julie Franklin, Jeremy Jones, Randy Mathena, Bob Ross, Rob Green, Neil and Gail Christian, Nick Hyduke, Tony and Emily Rackley, John Arrington, Roger Martin, Duwan Dunn, Janet Roberson Sumner, Mary Harris Edwards, Terry and Gerry Green, Jerry and Brenda Miller, Rob Schwinn, John Dannert and his brother, Kyle, Jerry Maxey, Tony Cicora, Vince Harris, Brian Blades, Scott Gould, Kimberly Kelly and the crew at WSPA, Glynn Zeigler, Sarah and Roy Gullick, Gene Dillard, Marty Winsch, Lee Landenberger and his family, Peter Cooper, Meredith Bost, Ray Guenthner, Robert Seilor, Leslie Garren Hart, Nicole Kelly, Fess Shelton, Joey Holmes, Ann Wicker, Karin Gillespie, Pat Jones and Debbie Knebel, Roger Rhoades, Roy Flurher, Carl Clegg, Wanda Lu Paxton, Darryl Holland, Marshall Chapman, Jay Spivey, Fabrizio Del Monte, Charlie Jennings, Mark and Lura Dye, James Shannon, Andy White, Lyn Riddle, the Lynn(e)s, Meg Barnhouse, Lisa Holton, Randy Coleman, Danny Crowe, Sydney Fanning, Bob Inglis, Katy Watts, Mary Miller, Margaret Gaulden, Frank Foster, Lavena Wilkes, Betsy Schroeder, Baker Maultsby, Jimmy Brehm, John Abdalla, Marty Kern, Keith Perissi, Matt Mayes, John Felty, Todd Shriver. I would also like to thank Beth Nissen, Glen Craney and David Martin. Thanks, too, to Dea, Linda, Elizabeth, Leslie and those very special friends who have kept us in their hearts and prayers—God knows I've needed them.

We've been fortunate to have supporters who've served as steadfast counselors, too, especially propping us up with their small-business acumen. Uwe Diestel, one of the most elegant gentlemen I've ever known, has helped us through his position at SCORE, the Service Corps of Retired Executives. He hooked us up with the Small

Business Development Center of South Carolina, where we got even more guidance, several financial projections and a sympathetic ear. Barry Starling, a onetime banker, financial consultant, friend and fan, also provided breathtaking brilliance in his analysis of and work on behalf of our little company.

Thanks wouldn't be complete without a shout-out to our staff. Great job. Really.

As for this book itself, Betsy Teter and Hub City have been a godsend in ways that Betsy will never know. Theresa Gioia served as my own personal intern at the start of this project, and her research, good cheer and great help proved more beneficial than she might see in these pages.

And to save the best for last, my most special thanks go to my brother, Stephen, for his profound role in all of this, and his wife, Melanie; to my sister, Sally, an abiding presence; and to my parents, Jack and Katherine, for everything. Huge thanks belong to Mary Dedinsky and Carlisle Herbert, who believed in us from the beginning and somehow still do. And loving thanks go to Dr. John Feagin, my uncle and godfather, for his counsel and concern, and to Irene Laughlin, for her care and love and for her daughter.

HUB CITY
PRESS

Hub City Press is an independent press in Spartanburg, South Carolina, that publishes well-crafted, high-quality works by new and established authors, with an emphasis on the Southern experience. We are committed to high-caliber novels, short stories, poetry, plays, memoir, and works emphasizing regional culture and history. We are particularly interested in books with a strong sense of place.

Hub City Press is an imprint of the non-profit Hub City Writers Project, founded in 1995 to foster a sense of community through the literary arts. Our metaphor of organization purposely looks backward to the nineteenth century when Spartanburg was known as the "hub city," a place where railroads converged and departed.

Recent Hub City Press Titles

Mercy Creek • Matt Matthews

Home is Where: An Anthology of African-American Poetry from the Carolinas • Kwame Dawes, editor

Waking • Ron Rash

The Iguana Tree • Michel Stone

The Patron Saint of Dreams • Philip Gerard

Middlewood Journal • Helen Scott Correll

Literary Dogs & Their South Carolina Wrters • John Lane and Betsy Wakefield Teter, editors